ORGANIZE YOUR HOME IN A YEAR OR LESS!

Your Complete Guide to Keep your House Under Control and Get Organized with Powerful Room by Room Organization Hacks in 12 Simple Exercises

By Kai M. Jordan

outlined in this book.

By reading this document, the reader agrees that under no circumstances is the author responsible for any losses, direct or indirect, that are incurred as a result of the use of the information contained within this document, including, but not limited to, errors, omissions, or inaccuracies.

Table of Contents

YOUR FREE GIFT

As a way of saying thanks for your purchase, I'm offering ***The Decluttering and Organizing Bundle*** for FREE to my readers.

This valuable package includes four valuable components:

1- The Decluttering Booklet (42 decluttering exercises + 22 self-reflection pages + inspirational quotes).

2- The Decluttering Journal & Planner (30-steps to Declutter your home).

3- The Ultimate Decluttering Checklist

4- Let Go of Clutter: Supply Checklist, and Stay the Course Worksheet

To get instant access just go to:

http://swenettbooks.com

or Just Scan this Code by Your Phone

Inside the bundle, you will get:

- 42 practical decluttering exercises in the book in a printable coloured nice format.
- 22 self-reflection pages in the book in a printable coloured format.
- 262 pages of Decluttering Journal in a bright watercolour design.
- Perfect 30-step plan for Decluttering your home.
- Ultimate Checklist for Decluttering which will save you hours of your decluttering time and skyrocket your productivity
- Let Go of Clutter: supply checklist.
- Stay The Course Worksheet.

If you want to get the maximum benefit through your organizing your home journey, make sure to grab the free bundle NOW!

* * *

INTRODUCTION

> *My goal is no longer to get more done, but rather to have less to do. – Francine Jay*

If you have been using my *Happy Decluttered Life* book series to declutter your home and your life, you might pick up this book. The first book in the series is entitled *Decluttering Your Home In A Year Or Less!* the second book is called *Declutter Your Mind In A Year Or Less!* the third book explains how to *Organize Your Digital Life* and do a digital detox. You might pick up this book if you have successfully decluttered your home. You believe that you're mentally prepared to take the next crucial step toward a joyful, decluttered life: effectively and efficiently organizing your home so that you, your family, and your spaces can function in symbiotic harmony. This means that not only should your area serve you by saving you time and space and giving you a peaceful place to relax, but you should also be able to reach a point where you can add positive energy to your space by organizing it in an optimum manner.

Regardless of your reason for picking up this book, if the introduction resonates with or inspires you to take back control of your life and your time, then you're ready to begin the exciting journey of organizing your home, your prized possessions and most importantly, your life. As per the lessons in my first three books in this series, decluttering is essential. The results are evident in the physical and mental sense of achievement after getting rid of the mountains of *stuff* you may have accumulated or inherited over the years.

However, even though decluttering your home and mind is a cause for celebration, a disorganized (albeit decluttered) home can cause similar stresses as a cluttered home. These stresses include:

- Conflict between partners or family members because they cannot find essential things such as clothes, papers, toys or sentimental items.
- Time-wasting or unnecessary delays caused by searching for items stored in inconvenient or inaccessible places in your home.
- The mental stress of looking at the disorganized

spaces in your home daily and not having the time to organize them in ways you would like.

These stresses can be overcome by following the method— which I've carefully curated from my personal experience with decluttering and organization—in this book.

* * *

ABOUT THE AUTHOR

Kai M. Jordan is an Amazon best-selling author in the field of self-development, home management and lifestyle coaching. Visit http://swenettbooks.com and get access to Kai's Decluttering Bundle for FREE.

In her books, Kai shares over ten years of practical knowledge and the timeless wisdom she learned from an early age about managing homes, mind and life by self-discovery and self-management. She turns these life lessons into actionable steps to help you develop a healthy relationship with yourself, others, and life itself.

In her honest and inspiring books, Kai talks about what she believes are the obstacles to living your desired life. She shares best practices to help you declutter your home, mind & life, improve powerful habits, erase negativity, control anxiety, reduce overthinking, and minimize any expectations of others. She guides YOU to think, decide and become the best version of yourself.

Kai studied business administration and project management. When she's not on her mission to make people's life better, she loves to read, meditate, workout, and take long walks in nature.

From Kai:

Before developing my method of home organization, there were many times in the past when I felt demotivated, lost and overwhelmed when I thought about tackling the task of organizing my home. My home was messy and disorganized and stressed me out daily. I had this nagging inner voice that would judge me for not having a pristinely organized home like the homes I saw around me or on social media. Having gone through the seemingly daunting experience myself, I realized that home management is not something to be intimidated by but something to embrace as a way of life and enjoy. I learned that organizing your home affords you peace of mind and quality time with your loved ones and grants your important possessions the respect they deserve by being correctly stored. Organizing my home meant I had more time to spend on the activities I truly valued, such as taking a relaxing hike, meditating, exercising, and cuddling up with a great book, instead of spending all my time cleaning and putting things away.

This book has been informed by my more than ten years of hands-on experience in passing on home management's positive mental and physical impact. Throughout your reading of this book, I would like you to remember that I had the same feelings of negativity and anxiety, comparing myself to others and overthinking as you before I began my journey of home organization. I am living proof that organizing your home can be achieved through implementing a few good habits; being open to being taught some important life lessons, and embracing the possibility of discovering new things about yourself—how you interact with the spaces in your home, and how to improve your decision-making skills and your life as a whole.

* * *

THE OBJECTIVES OF THIS BOOK

This book will inspire you to see the physical, mental, economic, and emotional value of having an organized home. You will see the value in respecting your spaces, possessions, and time through implementing practical tips and tricks to make organization a breeze instead of an intimidating tornado. Implementing the tips and strategies in this book will create tangible and intangible positive results for your home and you. Whether you're just starting to organize your recently decluttered home or looking for the organizing hacks that will make your already organized home even more convenient, this book will hold your hand through the process.

Since the previous book in the series explained how you can declutter your mind of negative thoughts related to your possessions, I will begin this book by showing you how to transform your mindset from one of decluttering to one of organizing. This means that a clear distinction between decluttering and organizing will be drawn, so you can rest assured that you and your home will not be appearing on the latest installment of *Hoarders: Buried Alive*. When you decide to transform your mindset, you will be able to identify what is holding you back from realizing your potential to organize your home.

The negative thoughts that can crop up when embarking on your home management journey will be briefly explored; it is essential to demystify the feelings and thoughts that might be holding you back in your organizing journey. Then, I will walk you through the crucial psychological tool known as the EQ Wheel to increase your self-awareness and self-appreciation and get your anxiety and possible negative feelings about organizing your home under control.

Next, we will explore how to build positive habits and routines relating to organizing your home and keeping it organized. The habits, routines, checklists and to-do lists you choose to implement to keep your house running like a well-oiled machine will largely depend on the structure of your family unit, your lifestyle, and the amount of time you dedicate to organizing. Developing the habit of regularly decluttering your spaces is step one; building your organizing skills and habits is step two, and diligent cleaning habits are step three to controlling your home and life.

You will find solutions to the seemingly 'bad' habits you may have developed about organizing your home. In this regard, it is essential to consider what type of organizer you are based on your personality. Organizing styles are highly relevant in your journey of self-discovery as you begin to organize your home.

After transforming your mindset and helping you develop healthy organizing habits and routines, the next logical step is to get you motivated about organizing your home! Procrastination is probably the most notorious thief of motivation, and I want to prove that you can overcome it. To do this, we will investigate how to implement the methods to overcome procrastination and link these methods to ways you can avoid procrastination when organizing your home.

Once you're motivated to get started and release your inner organization Formula One racer, I will establish a few basic principles and requirements to have at the ready before you start organizing your home. In setting out these basics, it is essential to consider standard methods, organizing systems, and themes used in the home management industry. This is because home organization and management is not a "one-size-fits-all" concept, and inspiration on what would work best in your home can be found if you seek it out.

Having established the basic principles of organizing, I will take you through how to organize every space in your home and show you "a whole new world" of convenience, time management, and peace of mind (flying magic carpet not included). There are various points or rooms where you can make your starting point, and the decision on where to start is essentially up to you; however, from my personal experience, I've chosen to take you through organizing your home in the following order, ranked by how often you use these spaces in your home:

- your kitchen (this includes your pantry, refrigerator, and freezer)
- your bathroom
- your living areas (this includes your living room, dining room, patio, backyard, kids' playroom, den and home office)
- your bedroom and closet (this include your jewelry, cosmetics, linen and shoes)
- our garage, basement, and attic and
- our sentimental items

Finally, I will provide helpful and easy-to-implement tips on maintaining your home impeccably organized. Maintenance includes reviewing the amount of *stuff* in a space at regular intervals—monthly or annually, for example—and involves effectively and efficiently cleaning these spaces. Hence, they stay clean without requiring an intense deep clean every week. Please note to do the organizing exercises at the end of each chapter. You can complete one exercise monthly to make this a year of progress.

Remember that "tidying your physical space allows you to tend to your psychological space." Therefore, we must begin by transforming your mindset from the goal of decluttering your space to organizing it (Hidlebaugh, 2022).

* * *

CHAPTER 1: ORGANIZE YOUR MINDSET

Decluttering Vs Organizing

Set peace as your highest goal and organize your life around it. –Brian Tracy

As you will have gathered from the titles and content of my first two books in this series, you have to start by decluttering your home before you can walk the path of organizing your home. A common misconception is that decluttering and organization are the same in a home. However, the difference between these two concepts is quite stark, and each involves different thought processes and exercises.

Simply put, decluttering your home involves "removing unnecessary, unused, unloved items" (Poplin, 2018). A decluttered home only contains what you want to keep or need as the occupant or owner. These would be the essential items that help you function every day or those that bring you joy, peace and happiness. Organizing your home can be defined as "creating a simple [storage] system...for items that you need, use, and love" (Poplin, 2018). An organized home is one where everything you need access to has its logical place, and the system implemented to manage each space is simple yet functional.

A simple example can illustrate the distinction between decluttering and organizing. You have recently completed the formidable task of decluttering your bathroom. You have decided to keep your child's toothbrush because it is an essential daily item they need access to. If your home is organized, you will ensure that the toothbrush lives in the bathroom and that your child understands your system of why their toothbrush should live in the bathroom. If your home is disorganized, your child might search for their toothbrush in the grocery cupboard. At the same time, you frantically consider sending out a search party to look for it to prevent your imminent mental breakdown from your child being late for school for the third time that week.

Stressful situations such as the one above can be easily avoided by understanding the following concept: decluttering is often a one-off task, but organizing is an ongoing process that requires maintenance and taking pride in your space. Decluttering and organizing requires considerable effort, mental strength and motivation; however, by implementing an organizing system suitable for your home, you will never feel as though you're starting from scratch every time you want to review the contents or organization of space in your home.

By already successfully decluttering, you have won most of the battle. That is something to celebrate because you have paired down the amount of stuff you have in your home and made important decisions about the possessions you value or require. This is a fantastic achievement, especially considering that studies show that "54% of Americans say that they feel overwhelmed with clutter filling up their homes" (Peysakhovich, 2022). This means that you haven't only proven to yourself that you respect your *stuff*, but you're now well on your way to showing how much you appreciate your *space*.

For example, during your decluttering process,

you may have considered downsizing the 60-inch flat-screen television you already had, but, in the end, you decided to keep it. This decision was hopefully motivated by how hard you worked to save up to buy that television and the fact that enjoying a good documentary is how you unwind after a long day. Your mindset regarding your television should have changed from wanting to get rid of it to deciding the value it adds to your life.

Now, as you begin organizing your home, your mindset has to shift further to managing the space around that television so it can continue adding value to your life in the way you want. Therefore, you wouldn't store your detergents or food items near your tv and risk damaging it.

Now that you understand the distinction between decluttering your home and organizing it, it is logical to identify the factors that might be holding you back from switching your mindset to one of organizing. Remember, the fact that you have less stuff and fewer items in your home is already an achievement in itself. We seek to take that achievement to the next level by organizing your home.

Reasons for a Disorganized Mindset

We've all been there. You're about to leave the house to head to work, but you can't find your phone or your house keys. Your stress level starts to increase because firstly, you're going to be late for work. Secondly, you start feeling that sense of dread from not being able to find something meaningful. Statistics show that the top five most commonly misplaced items in a home are shoes, keys, TV remotes, phones, and glasses (Peysakhovich, 2022). These items are not even clutter: they are essential items required for everyday life. Even though you may have misplaced some of these items in your home before, your anxiety, fear and lack of motivation when starting to organize your home are not lost.

Anxiety and stress related to disorganized spaces and not knowing where to begin is common. Surveys indicate that "57% of women have said that they have issues organizing their closets [and] this has added to their overall stress levels when trying to find things they need from their closets in a hurry" (Peysakhovich, 2022). This shows that you're not alone in the feelings of disappointment you might get when you open your pantry or closet to look for something you need immediately and can't seem to find the elusive item.

Other common reasons you might feel overwhelmed when thinking about organizing your home. Most of us have that inner voice that makes us doubt ourselves, our decisions, our goals, our abilities, and our progress. You could liken this inner voice to the sinister villain in every Disney movie who attempts to sabotage the hero at every opportunity. This so-called villain can manifest itself when you feel demotivated or overwhelmed at the thought of organizing your home. It also builds up the feeling of being crushed into a towering, multi-storey parking lot by making you think, perhaps, that you have to organize every room in your house in a week instead of taking it room by room at your own pace. The villain could be skulking around your mental space as you scroll through your social media feeds and making you feel inadequate about your organization skills. You justifiably want your home to be "Pinterest-perfect" or "Instagram-ready," but comparing yourself to others instead of being inspired or motivated by others will result in a negative attitude towards organizing. You might feel that you're just not good enough at getting your home to where you want it to be.

Another recent reason you might need to transform your mindset towards organizing is the COVID-19 pandemic.

The pandemic saw most of the world spending unpredictable months-on-end in isolation and lockdowns.

This means that many of us went from working in an organized office environment to being forced to recreate that space in our homes. It also saw many parents becoming teachers, as children had to be homeschooled; this required parents to create makeshift home classrooms.

Rooms previously used for storage in your home became prime real estate for either a home office or a home classroom. The items previously stored there had to either find a new home or be shoved somewhere else during the lockdowns. As a homeowner or occupier, you had to be creative and constantly modify your home to accommodate the various spatial difficulties that came with the pandemic.

Identifying the understandable and common reasons why you may not feel completely excited about organizing means there has to be a solution to overcome these negative feelings before you take on each room in your home. That solution lies in self-reflection and increasing self-awareness to determine what you want to achieve by organizing your home.

How to Transform Your Mindset

Truly believing that you can organize your home comes from learning how to increase your self-awareness and emotional intelligence. After doing so, you will understand that having an organized home affords you peace of mind, opportunities to be creative, and the ability to spend quality time on the things you genuinely enjoy.

Increasing your self-awareness can be achieved using a simple psychological tool or concept known as the *EQ Wheel* or *Emotional Quotient Wheel*. This tool helps you to understand more about yourself so you can respond to and communicate with those around you. Emotional intelligence is "the ability to sense, understand and effectively apply the power and acumen of emotions to facilitate higher levels of collaboration and productivity" (Justice and Target Training

International Ltd., 2021). The wheel is divided into four quadrants that indicate how you process situations within yourself and conditions about others. The four quadrants of the EQ Wheel are Self-Awareness, Self-Regulation, Social Awareness, and Social Regulation.

These concepts must be unpacked as we relate them to getting into the correct mental space to organize your home successfully.

***Self-Awareness*:** This is defined as your "ability to recognize and understand your moods, emotions and drives, as well as their effect on others" (Justice and Target Training International Ltd, 2021). Organizing your home would mean acknowledging that even though you would ideally like your home to remain clutter-free, life happens, and there may be times when clutter is inevitable. However, there are also steps you can take to manage this. One such method is accepting your *clutter ceiling,* which is your threshold or tolerance for a certain amount of clutter in a space. An example is the notorious "junk drawer" that most families seem to have in their kitchens.

A lack of self-awareness would lead you to either clean out this drawer daily or leave the junk within to accumulate until it becomes unmanageable. Increasing your self-awareness would mean acknowledging the existence of the junk drawer and coming up with a system where it is cleaned at least once a month or ensuring that the drawer has another purpose to prevent it from being filled with junk. Also, suppose you live with other people. In that case, self-awareness means acknowledging that everyone's possessions deserve their space in the home and that organizing without this might lead to emotional conflict with your household members. You must essentially recognize and limit the area you let your stuff take up.

***Self-Regulation*:** This quadrant is "the ability to control or redirect disruptive impulses and moods and the propensity to suspend judgment and think before acting" (Justice and Target Training International Ltd, 2021). In terms of home organization, this means making (sometimes difficult) decisions about where items in your home belong. Continuing with the junk drawer example, you may decide that the junk drawer is wholly off-limits and that the stuff placed in the drawer should be stored on your dining room table. However, this would be an eyesore, of course. This is an example of a learning experience: is the infamous junk drawer truly serving any purpose, or can the junk be eliminated and the drawer put to better use? Another example of Self-Regulation would be to adopt a system of "one in means one out" when reviewing the contents of your closet.

This means that when you buy a new item of clothing, you donate or get rid of an old article.

Social Awareness is "the ability to understand the emotional makeup of other people and how your words and actions affect others" (Justice and Target Training International Ltd, 2021). In a home management context, this would be especially important if you live with other people and have to consider their belongings when creating an organizing system in your home. An example of this would be to understand that your husband or son's Marvel figurine collection is not taking up space that other items could fill but rather that it is essential to that family member and should be stored in such a way.

Social Regulation: This concept is the "ability to influence the emotional clarity of others through a proficiency in managing relationships and building networks" (Justice and Target Training International Ltd, 2021). If we were to relate this to organizing a home, it would mean that because you have accepted your clutter ceiling and the space that your loved ones' possessions take up in your home and have acknowledged your decluttering progress, you will neither compare yourself to others and feel inadequate nor feel stressed about having guests in your home because organizing is a journey, not a destination.

A Goal-oriented Mindset

The aspects of the organizing journey you choose to focus on before you start organizing your home will determine whether this will be a walk in the park for you or whether you will always feel as if you're living in the shadow of unattainable ideals. The mindset of an organized person is a forward-looking one. It would help if you focused on the stuff you chose to keep during the decluttering process instead of looking back in regret at the things you gave away. Looking forward and viewing an organized home as your goal will automatically make you excited about starting the organizing process.

As stated in the opening quote of this Chapter, you must work backwards from the purpose of peace of mind when begining to organize your space. Mindfulness or the "basic human ability to be fully present, aware of where we're and what we're doing, and not overly reactive or overwhelmed by what's going on around us," is a concept that briefly explains the benefits of organizing your home (Mindful Staff, 2020). Work on transforming your mindset towards managing. You can change time into *quality time*, space into *the creative or peaceful area*, and decluttering into *a system*.

* * *

Key Takeaways from This Chapter

Before we delve into the next Chapter on building healthy home management habits and routines to avoid organizing becoming a chore, let's summarize how to transform your mindset from decluttering to organizing your home.

- Decluttering is a one-off process that involves getting rid of your unused or unwanted stuff. In contrast, organizing is a continuous process involving creating a system to conveniently and respectfully store the things you need and choose to keep after decluttering.

- Feeling overwhelmed, stressed, guilty or inadequate about organizing your home is extremely common and understandable, with COVID-19 creating additional stressors within the home environment.
- Overcoming a negative mindset towards organizing means understanding yourself and others better so that you make the right decisions for yourself, the people you live with, and your space.
- Adopting a goal-oriented attitude towards your home will help you envision and focus on the peaceful home you're striving for by organizing it.

* * *

EXERCISE #1

Focus On What You Kept

Date:____________

Write down ten items you are grateful you kept. What do they tell you about what your organizing goals are? Following through on this, write down five areas in your home that you want to get organized in the next year.

CHAPTER 2: ORGANIZING HABITS AND ROUTINES

> *We're what we repeatedly do. Excellence then, is not an act, but a habit. –Aristotle*

A 'habit' can be defined as "the tendency to do something, whether harmful or health-promoting" (Eatough, 2021). A 'routine' is "a series of behaviours frequently, and intentionally, repeated" (DePaul, 2021). Habits and routines form part of our daily lives. They appear as seemingly unconscious routines such as brushing our teeth in the morning and conscious or deliberate habits such as going for a morning run.

Habits and routines, incredibly when goal-oriented, can be highly beneficial to our physical and mental health by making us feel better about ourselves, helping us develop personally or professionally, and also reducing our feelings of anxiety. Examples of this are when we choose to create healthy eating habits, get into a routine of decreasing the amount of time we spend on our phones, or ensure that we make a habit of attending a social event at least once a month. Conversely, certain habits and routines can negatively impact our health or hinder our success. Such bad habits include smoking, procrastination, and creating clutter by buying items you don't need.

Developing good habits and routines for organizing your home can make you feel less overwhelmed and more in control of your daily life. A truly organized home can't exist without well-thought-out routines and habits.

A habit helps your brain methodically organize itself before you act or take on a task. This internal organization does not come naturally, and all of us must take steps to break bad habits or form brand new good ones.

In our investigation of ways to combat

procrastination, let's start by considering "The Three Ds of New Habit Formation," which can easily be used to develop helpful home management habits and routines (Tracy, 2007, p. 6). They are as follows:

You need three essential qualities to develop the habits of focus and concentration, which are all learnable: decision, discipline, and determination.

First, decide to develop the habit of task completion. Second, *discipline* yourself to repeatedly practice the principles you're about to learn until they become automatic. And third, back everything you do with *determination* until the habit is locked in and becomes a permanent part of your personality (Tracy, 2007, p. 6).

Unpacking the above three concepts about keeping your home organized will clarify the benefits of good habits within the home.

Decision: What Should I Stop Doing?

To develop good habits and routines to manage your home, you must acknowledge and eliminate the "bad" habits you might currently have. You need to actively decide to mentally purge yourself of these bad habits and replace them with new and better ones. Before you punish yourself for keeping that menacing junk drawer packed to the brim, there are a few everyday bad organizing habits that almost every homeowner is guilty of practicing. Don't panic if you can relate to a few bad habits identified by home organizers interviewed for *Reader's Digest Canada* in January 2022.

- Storing items that are hardly used in spaces that should contain frequently used items. For example, storing a large suitcase on an eye-level shelf instead of everyday clothing.
- Storing different items together: for example, storing cereals next to detergents.
- Keeping items you mean to donate in the corner of your house that soon becomes an unmanageable mountain.
- Leaving similar-looking items unlabelled. For example, storing unlabelled salt and sugar jars beside each other can lead to a morning disaster. Labelling items and containers will become something you rely on throughout your organizing journey. Consider investing in a labelling machine or personalize labels by sticking them on and handwriting them.
- Leaving received mail piling until it accumulates into an intimidating stack.
- Keeping items that you have already replaced or upgraded. This is especially common for smartphones and other electronic devices.
- Keeping reusable shopping bags in a drawer in your kitchen instead of your car, ready to go to the store with you.

- Failing to regularly sort receipts and other items in your purse, school bag, or work laptop bag.
- Making the chair in the corner of your bedroom a mini closet. This chair is often better dressed than the homeowner after various discarded outfit options or unfolded laundry have been flung at it. It should be treated as your very own throne of relaxation instead.
- Unnecessarily cluttering your nightstand with all of your toiletries, electronic devices, and reading material.
- Shopping for products to organize your stuff before deciding how you want to manage space. This bad habit is often compounded by buying more organizing containers than you need, then needing a place to store these containers.
- Fill every space to the brim without leaving breathing or growing room in case you need to add more items to that space later on.
- Failing to put things back where they belong, especially in spaces like the pantry, living room, and kitchen.
- Keeping expired items in your kitchen or bathroom that take up space can also be dangerous if you have children or elderly family members who might use these products without checking the expiry dates.

As you can tell from the above list, you're not alone in any bad organizing habits you might have. To progress, you need to make the active decision to drop these bad habits and replace them with more positive ones. How to develop new patterns will be explored when we determine *to stop* on this journey.

Discipline: What Should I Continue Doing?

Remember to be kind to yourself throughout this journey to an organized home. The fact that you want to get your house in order is already a step in the right direction. The fact that you have decluttered and have set aside items to be donated are achievements in themselves. Success at organizing does not require a complete overhaul of your personality because this is not only likely to cause you mental harm but is also unsustainable.

It would help if you made your organizing habits flow organically into your personality, family or home structure, and time availability. It would help if you built the habits and routines that work best for you. For example, if you live in a one-bedroom apartment with your partner; it makes sense to divide the home organization routines between you. Perhaps one of you handles the morning routine, and the other takes the evening one. However, this wouldn't work if you're a single working parent with three children; you would need to ensure that either your children do their part to keep their spaces organized if they're of an age where they're able to, or your organizing routine needs to be as fundamental as completing one task per day of the week. Other family structures that can vary the level of organizing habits are a two-parent home with children, a large extended family living under one roof, or a single person living alone.

Our free time depends on our careers, studies, and family commitments. People often say, "I just don't have the time to organize my home"; however, please note that humans choose to spend time on the things they love and value. Organizing your home will clear your mental clutter and make what it is that you genuinely love and value even more apparent to you. For example, you might prioritize going for a run after work over folding and putting away your laundry. A disciplined person would realize that completing both tasks are great habits to continue. An hour-long run could be reduced to 45 minutes, leaving 15 minutes to fold your laundry.

Organizing and maintaining an organized home does not mean you can't continue the other good habits and routines you have developed. The organization should be incorporated into your lifestyle in a way that is manageable for you.

Determination: What Should I Start Doing?

Watch your thoughts; they become your words; watch

your comments, they become your actions; watch your actions, they become your habits; watch your habits, they become your character; watch your character, it becomes your destiny. –Lao Tzu

Once you have decided what home management habits you would like to drop and which ones you already do that you would like to incorporate into your new home organization routine, you finally have to decide what habits you want to adopt or develop. As you embark on your journey of refining your home organization routine, you must keep your goal of peace of mind, more free time, and a neat home in mind. Being organized allows you room to breathe, think, and be creative. Indeed, remarkable or innovative things are sometimes created in chaos; however, this is rare, and most of us thrive in an organized environment.

To develop good home management habits, you must first keep in mind what you want to achieve by organizing your home, making getting into the routine much more manageable. Next, you must anticipate and prepare for a few bumps in the road. A spot could present itself as an urgent deadline that has cropped up at work and prevents you from spending as much time on organizing at home as you initially planned for that week. Let's explore five everyday speed bumps that could be preventing you from efficiently managing your home, as discussed by Erin Eatough, Ph.D., for the wellness blog, Better Up (Eatough, 2021).

1. **Your environment feels out of your control**. So, take control of the stuff in your home and set yourself up for success by ensuring that you have *less stuff*.
2. **You're attempting to change multiple habits simultaneously**. Avoid anxiety and being overwhelmed by transforming one lousy practice before moving on to the next.
3. **You're avoiding committing to changing your habits**. This can be solved by thinking about or writing down the benefits of changing old habits or routines or developing new ones.
4. **The outcome is overshadowing your view of the process**. Home organization is a journey and not a destination. The psychological processes you put yourself through while creating an organization system tailored to your home are not something that can be rushed. Your focus should be on the end goal of an organized home, but it shouldn't hinder the steps you take to get there. Remember to slow down, breathe, and remember that your journey will differ from the next person's.
5. **You believe that drastic changes make more of a difference than minor**

changes. Regardless of your family structure or busy lifestyle, it would be best if you always started with small tasks. This could be ensuring you check your fridge for expired food when taking out the trash each week or teaching your kids how to store their toys after playing with them. Small steps will still get you to the desired destination at your own pace. The cumulative results of your small efforts will speak for themselves, just like when you first took those steps to declutter your home.

Studies have shown that it takes between 18 to 254 days to form a new habit, whether good or bad (Lally, 2009). Set yourself up for success by acknowledging your bad habits. Always celebrate progress at every step, no matter how small you think it is, and be kind to yourself, especially when adopting these new organizational habits.

Lists and Habits: A Classic Friendship

Picture it: your favourite buddy cop film (likely from the 1980s). One of the cop characters in the movie is the renegade— unpredictable and always wants to disregard the rules and take the law into his own hands. The other guy is strait-laced, does everything by the book, follows the rules, and is the voice of reason. The rebellious cop can be likened to the unpredictability of expecting yourself always to follow your organizing routines and practice the good habits you planned to develop. On the other hand, the proverbial goody-two-shoes can be likened to the tools you use to keep yourself on the straight and narrow when it comes to organizing.

The most common tools to help you stick to your organizing routines and habits are physical reminders of what you need to do daily. These reminders can be created in various forms such as checklists, to-do lists, marked calendars, dry erase boards, chalkboards, colour-coded chore lists, vision boards, mobile phone applications, and even post-it notes stuck on furniture.

The tools you use to stick to your organizational routine should be appropriate for your home, family structure, time availability, and lifestyle. They must be maintainable and shouldn't require a NASA instruction manual to update. Remember always to keep it simple enough for a child to understand. I've personally used colours, chalkboards, and calendars to my advantage in my home and seen excellent results. You and your kids will love decorating your schedules, which makes you all take pride in keeping your home organized per your family brand.

* * *

Key Takeaways from This Chapter

Next, we will unpack how to conquer procrastination when organizing your home. Let's take stock before proceeding. Taking stock is another healthy habit, especially before buying groceries!

- Effective habit building requires three steps:
  - Deciding which home (mis)management habits you should give up.
  - Being disciplined about not changing who you are intrinsical while incorporating better habits into how you organize your home.
  - Approaching new habits with determination, reasonableness, and your end goal in mind to motivate you.
- Lists, calendars, reminders, and other similar tools will help you maintain your home, keep control of your life, and set you up to succeed with your new home organization routine.

* * *

EXERCISE #2

Create a Schedule Right Now

Date:____________

Think about the organizing tasks you put off doing during your work week. Write them down in a list, and next to each, write down how long you think the job would take to complete.

Hooray! You've just created your first organizing schedule.

CHAPTER 3: OVERCOMING PROCRASTINATION

> *You don't have to see the whole staircase, just take the first step. – Martin Luther King Jr.*

Procrastination is a practice almost everyone is guilty of. Most of us have experienced that inevitable wave of stress that consumes us after we've put off a task until the very last minute, made some questionable decisions, and justified our choices with excuses that read like the second act of a Shakespearean tragedy. These excuses might include the notoriously misguided "I work well under pressure." You might believe that you're too busy, lazy or unmotivated, or you might be that person who gets distracted by a new task before completing the one at hand. Regardless of what house of procrastination you have been sorted into, you need to know that this Sorting

Hat may not always be correct, and you can remove it.

So, you're still feeling overwhelmed about organizing your home, and this is leaving you demotivated. You constantly put off the task as your *stuff* stares back at you while you try to relax. You're not alone in this feeling. Statistics show that "66% of Americans have admitted feeling stressed and anxious when their home is dirty or unorganized" (Peysakhovich, 2022). Being behind on completing tasks does not reflect on you as a person because no one can ever truly and completely catch up with the never-ending list of things on their to-do list.

As writer Edward Young once said, "procrastination is the thief of time" (St. John, 2015). This is even more true when it comes to organizing your home. The ultimate goal of having an organized home is peace of mind, a home you can take pride in, and free time to do the things you enjoy. We spend time on the things we care about, and you shouldn't be punishing yourself if organizing your spaces is not something you *want* to spend time on.

It is, however, something you *need* to spend some time on if you want to achieve that elusive peace of mind. If procrastination is the brick wall standing between you and the motivation to start organizing, then wind your feelings of inadequacy and unproductiveness into the rope you're going to throw over that brick wall to allow me to help you over it.

Eat That Frog!

"The ability to concentrate single-handedly on your most important task, to do it well, and to finish it, is the key to great success" (Tracy, 2006, p. xii). Procrastination is the leading cause of feeling too demotivated to complete tasks. However, instead of punishing ourselves for procrastinating, we should embrace it, own it and make some good decisions about how we choose to *wear* or process our procrastination.

We will never have the time to complete every task we need at home, socially, at school or work. This means that we will be in a perpetual state of procrastination if we don't change our mindset and decide to take control of what is within our reach in our lives. The same thought process applies to organizing your home. Starting the process of organizing involves accepting that you might always be motivated to do so as you make your way through each space in your home. The method also considers that organizing your home is an ongoing activity. Adopting the philosophy of eating that frog means completing your most difficult and time-consuming task before taking on any other because:

...if the first thing you do each morning is to eat a live frog, you can go through the day with the satisfaction of knowing that that is probably the *worst* thing that will happen to you all day long (Tracy, 2006, p. 2).

I will unpack a few simple methods for overcoming procrastination and link them to becoming and staying motivated about organizing and managing your home. These methods can be used individually or combined. You have to find what motivates you and apply it to how you organize your home. As we delve into each method, remember two important tips: first, you must prioritize the most significant or most challenging task to be done, and secondly, always keep your goal in mind.

The Methods

<u>Make Your Goal Clear:</u> This method involves visualizing and writing down your productivity goal to make it clear to yourself—clarity results in taking steps which result in productivity. You would do this by writing down your goal weight when beginning a weight-loss journey. The same applies to organizing your home. Set a goal of perhaps organizing one room per month or spending two hours on managing per day. Use colours, a vision or mood board, or make your dream the daily mantra you repeat to yourself when you wake up in the morning.

Plan Ahead: "Time management is *life* management, personal management. It is taking control of the *sequence of events*. Time management is having control over what you do next" (Tracy, 2006, p. 23). Taking the time to think ahead and set your intentions in detail can significantly save time. So, instead of waiting until you get home (understandably exhausted) from work to decide what organizing task you want to take (understandably none), create a monthly, weekly, or daily schedule for yourself to tackle those small tasks in the house.

Prioritize the Big Fish That Will Feed Many: While you should start easing yourself into organizing by taking small steps to achieve your goal, this does not mean prioritizing smaller tasks over more important ones. For example, you should prioritize organizing your refrigerator before you tackle labelling family photographs or categorizing office supplies. The fridge is a high-priority task because you use it multiple times a day. Organizing family photographs, while also necessary, is not going to immediately improve your daily life as much as an organized refrigerator would.

Think About What Happens if You Don't Do It: A bricklayer wouldn't start laying a foundation of bricks without knowing what he will be building. Similarly, it would be best if you adopted a big picture mindset to organize your home to decide which brick or task is the most important. Considering your future of being late for work tomorrow if you fail to organize your closet today is a way of motivating yourself to get it done.

Procrastinate Creatively: Instead of the internal excuses we often make for procrastinating, use these to your advantage by leaving the low-priority tasks for later and focusing on the high-impact tasks. This would mean avoiding the disorganized gift wrap rolls in your garage until you have organized your bathroom into a fully functional space.

Rank Each Task by Priority: This is a fool-proof method to prioritize tasks that *need* to be done over jobs that you would *prefer* to complete. For example, if you're creating a schedule for when you get home from work, starting by unpacking the dishwasher or folding your laundry would set you up with spare time to attend to other lower-priority tasks. Take immediate action on that highest priority task as soon as possible.

Do What Necessary First Is: With this method, you should take control of what you're supposed to do and focus on getting it done. This method can effectively beat procrastination in a family or multi-person household. Tasks can be shared and remain the responsibility of the person allocated to them. The same goes for the other end of the spectrum if you're living alone, where if you don't organize your pantry, no one else will do it. Remember to celebrate progress at every turn, whether in the form of your favourite meal or curling up with a great book once your task is complete.

Prepare for All Possible Outcomes Before You Start: In an organizing context, this would mean assessing the space and planning out how you would like to organize it, sourcing the best storage materials, further decluttering if required, and celebrating that you're about to realize your vision for that space. Remember to focus on clarity when planning to organize.

Complete One Task At a Time: It would be impossible and demotivating to plan to organize your entire home in one day. You're setting yourself up for failure before you even begin. Tackle that high-priority task one step at a time. If you choose to start by organizing your clothes, start with socks if that is what gets you in the mental space to seek progress.

Upskill Yourself: Being unable to find your confidence, motivation or niche in organizing can be cancerous to progress. If you take the stance that you have some skills that can be applied to organizing your home, you will succeed in honing those skills. Be humble; ask your friends who have pristinely managed homes how they do it; or take inspiration from blogs and online tutorials. Successful organizers should inspire you, but you should avoid trying to *be* them because this causes those feelings of inadequacy and anxiety to creep back in.

Know Your Areas of Improvement: Consider the limitations you're placing on yourself (internal constraints) and the rules set on you (external conditions) regarding the organization. Are you convincing yourself that you need an untidy environment to remain creative or that an organized home is an easily attainable goal? The problem might be external to you because you work shifts and don't always have the time to complete your daily organizing routine—work at eliminating those constraints. Be kinder to yourself and give yourself less to do if it means more will be done.

Work Well Under Pressure: This method works if you subdivide your high-priority tasks into a few smaller lessons and knock them off your list. Creating mini-deadlines within a task can be extremely helpful. For example, if you're about to organize your kitchen, divide it into organizing the pantry, refrigerator, freezer, and stove areas. This way, you're guaranteed to see results and achieve progress.

Use What You're Good At: Try to get into organizing at your own pace and at the time of the day when you know you're most productive. Motivate yourself to work during the time or session you have allocated to achieve a task. Sometimes you need to pause, rest, and return to that pile of unsorted office stationery after a few hours with a fresh perspective. Minor setbacks should be used as opportunities to regroup and try out something different. Organizing is not a sprint but a marathon where planning and endurance are required.

Put Your Cell Phone Away: This is something we're all guilty of. You go to Pinterest to look for organizational inspiration and end up mining for memes, or you spend two hours replying to work emails. You need to actively *choose* to leave your phone aside until you complete your task. It sounds simple, but it is becoming increasingly more complex with corporate demands and our lack of free time. Use technology to make you a more efficient organizer, and don't let it control you or your time.

Focus on Each Task on Its Own: If you're organizing your kitchen cupboards, don't stop or give up until every counter is clear of stuff meant to go into those cupboards. Of course, stop, regroup, and return even more motivated if you're fatigued or reached a mental block.

* * *

Key Takeaways from This Chapter

As we progress into some essential home organization basic principles, we should review what we've learned about overcoming procrastination, staying motivated, and eating the giant home management frogs first!

- Justifying your reasons for procrastination is common, and almost everyone does it with work, home, and school-related tasks.
- Don't punish yourself for procrastinating about organizing your home; instead, own it, and find ways to use it to your advantage.
- The most effective ways to emerge from a slump of demotivation related to home management are prioritization of your most essential tasks, visualizing your end goal, and taking a step to start *today*.

- Procrastination can be overcome using various methods, which require you to be your life coach, motivator, and support system during those productivity slumps.

* * *

EXERCISE #3

Cancel Out Procrastination

Date:___________

Write down three excuses or reasons you use to justify your procrastination. Next to each excuse, write a method for you to apply from my list that will replace the excuse with action.

CHAPTER 4: THE ORGANIZING BASICS

For every minute spent in organizing, an hour is earned. –Benjamin Franklin

Laying the Foundation

Organization and home management are processes during which you will learn a lot about yourself. Remember, being disorganized does not define you as a person. It does not define your abilities to be a good person, parent, partner, or child. Instead, disorganization is a state that can be easily changed by laying a proper foundation of fundamental principles that you can apply and maintain in your home. It is essential to use the lessons described in the previous chapters about changing your mindset, building solid habits and routines, and staying motivated to develop your organizing foundation on positive energy. You are maintaining feelings of self-doubt and inadequacy when organizing will affect your decision-making abilities. Organizing with a negative mindset can be likened to a bricklayer laying a brick without first putting down some cement to secure it. You must ensure that your mind is as strong as a stable structure that you can build upon later. Part of laying that essential foundation of organization basics is determining your organizing style to decide the best approach for getting your home in order.

Different Organizing Styles

The Everything Out: These are visually focused people who need to see and be able to touch their stuff to feel in control. They will often avoid putting their things away until they've completed the task that requires the property. This organizing style can result in piles of stuff and cluttered space, making it difficult to think clearly. Such persons feel secure in seeing their stuff around them to avoid forgetting about it or failing to use it. People with this organizing personality should seek to use clear or colour-coded storage, shelving, or priority containers to organize their space.

The Nothing Out: These individuals prefer clear counters and not seeing their stuff to feel like they're in control. They believe that a clear mind requires a clear space, which often results in their stuff being hidden without being organized into a system. Aesthetically pleasing and digital methods of the organization usually help these personality types.

The Minimalist: This person is usually a perfectionist who avoids accumulating stuff unless it is necessary. They typically have a highly complex organization system that can sometimes lead to over-organizing. People with this organizing style can usually improve by acknowledging and considering the other organizing personalities in their homes.

The Straightener: These individuals prefer neat piles and straight lines to feel in control. They're notorious for insisting on organizing someone else's space before tackling their own. They tend to keep stuff and straighten or neaten it instead of considering the actual need or use of the object.

The Saver: They believe in simply keeping stuff because it might be used someday. They're also conscious of the money they might have spent on an item. These items include clothes, appliances, hobby items, and stock-piled food items. These personality types need to recognize their "clutter ceiling," regularly declutter their spaces, and adopt the system of discarding one thing when they bring in a new one.

The Fundamentals of the Foundation

Now that you have determined your organizing personality, my method of asking yourself four simple questions can be applied as you assess each space to be organized. Asking these questions before you begin will set you up for success and ensure that you have considered all possible roadblocks to the process. I will use this method to give you various practical tips on organizing each space in your home in the coming chapters. The fundamental questions are as follows:

- What is the challenge?
- What do I *need* from the space?
- What do I *want* from the space?
- What action should I take to achieve this?

Brick One: What Is the Challenge?

Ask yourself about your mindset and the space holding you back from organizing it. The challenges you run into before you start organizing could be that you need to do a bit more decluttering in a space. You might also be struggling to rid yourself of a few of those pesky lousy organization habits that we're all guilty of, as mentioned in Chapter 2. The challenge could be that you have never attempted to organize space or that you need to maintain or review the organizing system you're currently using.

Despite the challenges you might be facing, it is essential to remember that you're in control of the space. The space, or the stuff in it, shouldn't control you. If you're feeling overwhelmed, it's time to take back your power over those spaces and decide how they should be organized.

Brick Two: What Do You Need?

Consider exactly how you expect the space to function. Does the area need to be accessible to all household members, like a kitchen or bathroom? Are there commonly used items in the distance?

Does the space need to serve multiple functions, such as a home office and a storage room? Does the area need to be functional for a disabled or older adult? We require these potential needs in a space, and our needs speak directly to the space's function.

You must consider your spatial needs holistically when assessing any space. By this, you must consider your time constraints, such as whether you're on a deadline to get the room organized; your budget constraints; and whether you need to source additional storage materials.

It would help if you were economical when arranging, and buying fancy storage containers will not only hurt your budget but will also not magically solve your organizing issues. You still have to decide what goes into those fancy containers, which must be neatly organized.

Brick Three: What Do You Want?

Some may think your wants and needs for space are the same, which is a misconception. Your needs for a room can be defined as how the area has to function in your home. For example, your bedroom needs to be a neat place where you get ready for your day and sleep. Your wants for a space can be defined as what you ideally envision the area. This could be interpreted as the energy for the room, the colour scheme, the general aesthetic, or simply ensuring that the space does not return to a state of clutter.

If you don't have enough space to store what you have, you might have too much. Therefore, to achieve what you *want* in the area, you might need to declutter further and get rid of stuff you don't need. Storage space and storage containers can be found in almost every corner of your home, and they come in shoe boxes, unused containers and lids, and cleaned-out food tins. It would be best if you also got into the habit of donating or selling any new items that are of value or that can be used by someone else. You can truly achieve the aesthetic you want by using what you already have in your home.

Brick Four: Taking Action

To achieve what you need and want from your space, you must implement your intentions. Taking action requires an organizing system and, secondly, a theme that forms part of the organizing system. The design should be determined by the organizing personality category you fall into, and the system will then inform the theme.

For example, if you're organizing your pantry, you would plan that everyday items are stored on eye-level shelves, and unhealthy snacks are stored above eye level, so they're not easily accessible. The theme you select could be to categorize the everyday items according to their brand and to keep the snacks according to the colour of their packaging.

Organizing Systems and Themes

Simply put, you need an organizing system within every space you organize in your home. Simplicity is essential; the less complicated the system, the easier it is to maintain. Start by grouping similar items into categories. Depending on your organization, you will need broad categories and sub-categories within your system.

Then, decide on a theme, place the items into appropriate storage bins, and finally maintain the plan regularly to avoid it getting disorganized again. The most accessible music to use is colour. You can arrange your items according to the colours of the rainbow or from light to dark to organize spaces and make them visually appealing.

Any organizing systems you choose can be easily adapted or modified to any room in your home. You can categorize your stuff by colour, type, brand, condition, age, accessibility, frequency of use, or owner. Regardless of your organization system, it *has* to work for you, your family, or your co-habitants. It must be sustainable, simple, and bring you peace of mind.

Where to Start

The most common question the readers have

always asked me of my first two books in this series is "Where should I start?" My answer is always that you should start organizing by categories instead of by spaces. My preferred type, to begin with, is clothing, which includes your closet and dressing area. We need access to most of our clothing every day, and if your clothes are hard to find or hard to put away, that makes life more difficult.

The first and most crucial step is to declutter your clothing, which you have hopefully already done according to my book *Declutter Your Home In Less Than A Year*. If you choose to start with clothes, my method is straightforward: take everything out, put everything in front of you, and try every single piece. If it doesn't fit you, or you don't feel good about yourself when wearing it, ask yourself why it is still in your house. Multiple bars in your closet, middle shelves, and drawer dividers could potentially multiply your storage space.

You could also start with the "entrance area" or foyer of your home because this is the first or last area you see when you enter or leave your home. This might be easy to start because you need to keep organized and dedicated space for your keys, hats, shoes, scarves, coats, purses, masks, and anything you want to hang when you first enter your home or take with you before going outside. Not having these items organized might make you late in the mornings because you're trying to find things. This will set an ominous tone for the rest of your day. One of the most under-utilized spaces in our homes is the front door itself! You can hang some organizers on the door to create a permanent home for the items required at your entrance. Using the back of your entry is a life-changing tip because it keeps any counter and floor space near the door clear and makes you feel ready for the day because you can grab whatever you need.

Your home office or your creative workspace can also be where you start organizing. A portable cart beside your desk at the same height as yours would make the perfect home for everything on the desk. This keeps your desk clear and tidy, so you can get some work done!

My final category suggestion to start with is the 'paper' category. It is common for bills, kids' artwork, flyers, junk mail, etc., to accumulate and get stuffed into random drawers. The secret to organizing papers in your home is to separate them into five categories and file them to ensure they never get mixed up. I will elaborate on these five categories when I discuss how to organize your home office.

The 'food' category or the kitchen is another suggested starting point. This is the first space I will help you organize in the next chapter. At a high level, I suggest you move things around until your counters are empty. Labelling will save your life in the kitchen and ensure you never drink the salty coffee again! The same categories of food or goods should be stored together. Organizing your kitchen will be explored in greater detail in the next chapter.

If your goal is to organize your home in less than a year, then I recommend you spend an entire month organizing each space. Start small and allocate chunks of time to the process instead of expecting yourself to manage three rooms in one day and then feeling disappointed when you don't achieve this unattainable goal. A month per room will allow you to think about what you want for each space, make the necessary purchases to achieve it, get set into and organize it, and also give you time for any hiccups that might occur along the way.

* * *

Key Takeaways from This Chapter

In the next chapter, we will keep our foot on the accelerator and head straight into how to organize your kitchen and its various zones. A quick recap of what we've learned in this chapter is required. However,

- Before organizing, you need to lay a proper foundation for your organizing plan by determining which type of organizing personality you match the most.
- A proper assessment of each space is required before organizing it, and you need to ask yourself these four essential questions about the space:

  - What is the challenge?
  - What do I need from the space?
  - What do I want from the space?
  - What action should I take to achieve this?
- Once you have assessed the space, you must decide on an organizing system and a theme to ensure that the space functions and looks how you want it to.
- The space you choose to start your organizing journey largely depends on your organization goals and what space you choose to prioritize.

* * *

EXERCISE #4

Your Organizing Style

Date:____________

What type of organizing personality style do you think most fits you? Write down some habits that make you think you fit into that category. Next to each routine, write down an organizing or storage option you think would work to break this habit.

CHAPTER 5: ORGANIZING YOUR KITCHEN

I want my home to be that kind of place–a place of sustenance, a place of invitation, a place of welcome. – Mary DeMuth

I've chosen to start by helping you organize your kitchen because I firmly believe that the kitchen is the heart or core of the home. Regardless of your family structure at home, the kitchen is where most of us start and end our day. You either stumble in there in the morning to ensure you're fully human after enjoying your morning coffee, or you're there at dawn preparing breakfast and lunches for your family. At the end of a hard day, the kitchen is where you prepare the family dinner, help with washing up or grab a quick bite before returning to those pesky work emails.

A kitchen is a place that all of us use pretty often. For some of us, a kitchen is a therapeutic place where activities like baking or trying out new recipes help us focus on something other than work. For others, it is a learning ground where you're either learning to cook or teaching your kids how to avoid chopping their fingers off when cutting vegetables. In most cultures worldwide, that sense of togetherness and belonging can be found in sharing traditional or home-cooked food.

Memories that build the foundations of who we are often originate in the kitchen. Your use of the kitchen comes into play with almost every significant social event throughout the year, be it dinner parties, Christmas lunch, birthdays, kids' playdates, or wedding anniversaries.

A kitchen *must* be clean and be able to be easily deep cleaned regularly because it is used so often in multiple ways. A well-organized kitchen ensures that the highest standard of hygiene is maintained in this significant space. Organizing your kitchen according to your needs will give you the efficiency and functionality found in Anna Olson's test kitchen while allowing you to be as stylish, creative, and chic as Nigella Lawson.

What Are Your Challenges?

Close your eyes and imagine that you're Gordon Ramsay. Yes, you read that correctly. Imagine you're the hot-headed Scottish super-chef on an episode of his famous show *Kitchen Nightmares*. Now, look around your kitchen with your critical eye, and try to identify the challenges preventing you from organizing your kitchen according to your desired standard. Assess your kitchen and consider precisely what is holding you back from achieving your organizing goal in this space. Most importantly, remember that none of these challenges make you, as Ramsay would say, an "idiot sandwich" because they can be easily overcome!

Start your Ramsay-style kitchen walk-through by considering how the food in your kitchen is organized in your pantry, refrigerator, and freezer. Is there any expired food lying around that you're reluctant to get rid of or were unaware of? Are there jars of unidentifiable substances or random leftovers lurking in the back corners of your refrigerator that you avoid making eye contact with every time you open it? The freezer often becomes a dumping ground of food we need to keep frozen or portioned out, which turns into piles of food we intend to use but never do. Is the food in your freezer stacked by date or by size? We usually have similar habits in the pantry, and we buy grocery items just because we failed to check on what was already there.

Besides the financial loss you can experience from a messy kitchen; you can also experience a loss of prime real estate in your kitchen, put, *space*. Your kitchen might be on the smaller side, and as you assess it, you might notice that every single counter is full of stuff; appliances, food, pots, pans, and decorative items you want in your kitchen. Precariously stacked pots and dishes create access and storage problems. You're essentially facing the challenge of wanting more space instead of putting the area you have to use better. A small kitchen is still a kitchen and can function like an industrial kitchen if you implement the practical tips I will soon discuss.

Another challenge could be that your kitchen has to be functional for everyone in your household: your partner, parents, children, and maybe even your pets. Toddlers usually have their plastic cutlery and crockery that needs their own home. You might want to start a healthy eating journey, but there are snacks all over the kitchen that lead to temptation. Your detergents might be stored under your sink, but you have young children, making this unsafe. These challenges are common and inform what you need in your kitchen.

What Do You Need?

A further step to assessing how to organize your kitchen is to decide how to divide it up into zones. These zones are the areas you need in your kitchen to function and bring value to your life. For example, the corner of a counter on your kitchen island that is being taken up by appliances or kitchen gadgets you bought with the hope of using them 'soon' is not something you *need*. It would help if you were brutally frugal with your space while keeping it functional.

Most kitchens require the following zones: the grocery cupboard or pantry, the food preparation area, refrigerator and freezer area, kitchen cabinets, countertops, kitchen drawers, the sink, the dishwasher, and the stove area. The organizing system you choose for each zone must be suitable for you and your lifestyle and be easy to understand for the rest of your household.

Remember to assess your kitchen space before buying extra storage bins or installing additional shelving. With shelving, measure the maximum height you need using the tallest box or container you intend to store on these shelves.

A functional kitchen contains a food storage system that preserves the freshness of the food stored within and where expired food is visible and can be easily discarded.

In this regard, you might need to cater to various dietary requirements within your family, and your food storage system needs to cater to that. It would help to consider how available food is stored in the pantry, refrigerator, and freezer. You may prefer to buy certain products in bulk if you have a big family, so your organizing system needs to provide for either storing these items or having sufficient storage containers to decant the products and keep the remainder.

There are a few essential appliances that I would suggest purchasing to make the daily operations in your kitchen run smoothly. A dishwasher saves water instead of washing each dish; it also sterilizes your words and saves you heaps of time. A hand or stick blender is cheaper than most of the large and bulky blenders that take up so much valuable space in your kitchen, and it does the same job as its larger counterpart. These appliances are not a must, but they make things more convenient and economical for your financial and spatial budget. You might want to add them to your Wishlist as you move from considering your needs in your kitchen to your wants.

What Do You Want?

An aesthetically pleasing kitchen is something that most of us want. Your desired aesthetic can vary depending on your organizing personality style. You might wish for a minimalist kitchen style where your stuff is strictly limited to the things you need daily and nothing more.

Another aesthetic option is ultra-modern, where your pots and pans hang from the ceiling or are pinned to the wall, complete with clean lines, visible counter space, and slick appliances with the same colour scheme. You might favour the practical over the clinical (or your young children might have automatically made this decision) regarding the accessibility of the stuff in your kitchen—and for your kitchen to have that homely, warm, and lived-in feeling.

Your Wishlist for organizing your kitchen should be tempered to favour function over form. If your budget allows it, you can get those matching appliances you have been eyeing or that fancy rotating spice rack you saw on your favourite blog. My advice is to first deal with the essential needs of your kitchen by constantly considering the cleanliness, simplicity, and functionality.

Once you have the essentials sorted, you can let your creative juices flow and add in those special touches that make your kitchen a unique and creative space for you.

Taking Action

Now that you have zoned out your kitchen into the required sections, it is time to get busy and start organizing this space. At the outset, a two-step ladder should be kept in your kitchen to easily access those items that are stored higher than you can reach.

Grocery cupboard or pantry: A great way to organize your pantry is to envision a supermarket and how things are grouped. This will give you great organization and aesthetics. You would use the same organizational principles to organize a walk-in pantry, a grocery cupboard, or a pull-out pantry. Firstly, keep similar items together. For example, store all condiments, all spices, all types of pasta, all cereals, all flours or rice, all oils, etc. Next, I would advise that canned foods be stored together and categorized within their different groups, such as canned tomatoes, canned beans, etc. Investing in a sturdy spice rack or even a lazy Susan that rotates or is multiple-tiered can be a great way to store your spices and condiments. Snacks in the pantry can be grouped by their type (e.g., potato chips vs cookies) or by their frequency of use (e.g., occasional junk food is stored separately from regular healthy snacks).

You can organize the containers or items by their colour, brand, or how often you reach for them within each category. Remember to use vertical space effectively, and don't forget about those higher shelves. Use higher brackets to store additional stock of grocery items, toilet paper, extra beverages that don't fit in the fridge, or any items you don't need daily. Tempting, unhealthy snacks, your beer cooler or picnic basket can also be stored here.

The items at eye level should be used most often in your kitchen. I recommend hanging a chalkboard or dry-erase board on the back of your pantry door, with some chalk or markers nearby. Use this to write down a pantry item you have run out of as soon as it runs out. If you choose to decant items you have bought in bulk, remember to label and date the containers you decant them into using an erasable marker.

The food preparation area: Hygiene is most important because food gets easily contaminated by bacteria. Having a few different-coloured cutting boards each for meat, fish, and vegetables is helpful to avoid contamination if you need to cut multiple items for one meal. If you use a knife block, ensure it is regularly washed and that only clean and dry knives are placed in it. Keep a spray bottle of sanitizer or a container of sanitizer wipes near your food preparation area so that you can quickly wipe it down before and after preparing food.

Refrigerator: This is a zone that quickly gets untidy. Old food can accumulate and become unmanageable. Separate your refrigerator into zones to avoid having a significant cleanout every week. Use the refrigerator door for sauces, milk, beverages, and eggs. Use one shelf for condiments such as mayonnaise, pickles, and jams. Use another frame for dairy products such as cheese, butter, cream, and yogurt. Another shelf can be used for packed lunches or other "food prep" items for you to grab and go. The vegetable cooler drawer should strictly be used for fruits and vegetables. Most importantly, however you organize your refrigerator, please leave a shelf free solely for leftovers! This was a life-changing realization for me and ensured I would never find random food in the back of my refrigerator again.

Freezer: This is probably the most accessible space in the kitchen to zone out and organize. If you have a chest freezer, it would be advisable to store everything in clear storage containers or reusable plastic bags and be strict about labelling and dating everything. If you have an upright freezer, take one shelf for each food type. For example, I organize my freezer in my house with the top shelf reserved for ice and frozen treats. The next shelf is for frozen bread items like loaves, bread rolls, or frozen pizza (save money and freeze store-bought bread for later use). Next come the frozen vegetables, plant-based foods, and vegetables I've pre-cut for later use. The next shelf is for frozen snack-like foods and breakfast foods such as hot dogs, bacon, frozen pies, chicken nuggets, hamburgers, and anything else you can cook by popping them into the oven or air fryer. The next shelf is reserved for meat, including beef, mutton, and pork. Ensure that these are in plastic bags or containers to avoid cross-contamination. Next comes the raw chicken shelf (it is essential to dedicate a shelf to chicken due to the dangers of cross-contamination with any other foods). The last shelf should contain frozen fish and other seafood items. This method is fool-proof and makes packing that haul of groceries after you return from your tiring shopping trip a breeze.

Kitchen cabinets: Cabinets are often under-utilized spaces. Store like items together. This means storing the following items by category: all glasses, all mugs, all plates, all bowls, all appliances, all unique occasion dinner sets, all pots and pans, and all food containers. If your cabinets are deep, store the most commonly used items upfront. If they're high, keep the most used items lower. Pots and pans are a common storage hassle for many. Installing a few swing-out shelves in your cabinets will give you multiple storage levels. If you have a small kitchen, use your cabinet doors as additional storage. Stick a few adhesive hooks or thin racks using double-sided tape to store delicate items like rolls of foil, unused trash bags, plastic wrap, or your folded dishcloths.

The location of things should make sense. For example, pots and pans should be stored near the stove and plates, and serving dishes should be held near the food preparation area. Store your detergents and a few household tools like a hammer, spanner, and screwdriver in the cabinets under your sink. Detergents may need to be stored higher if toddlers are in the home.

Kitchen drawers seem to transform into dreaded junk drawers if no system exists. Invest in some drawer organizers or divided trays or reuse other storage containers you have hunted around the house to create sections within these drawers. Create an area or a whole drawer strictly for cutlery you use every day, another for larger serving spoons, another for special occasion cutlery, another for small appliances that can fit in these drawers, and one for any special cutlery or crockery that toddlers might require (if you have young children). Separate forks, knives, tablespoons, teaspoons, whisks, spatulas, wooden spoons, and barbecue tongs so they can be found easily, without digging up the entire drawer.

Countertops: These are prime real estate, and, depending on your organizing style, you can decide to keep them bare or curate their appearance with miscellaneous items that make your kitchen one-of-a-kind. You can create a tea and coffee station complete with matching tea, coffee, and sugar jars; a kettle; espresso machine; and a few signature mugs. A breakfast station is another option for your family to gather, grab, and go on those busy mornings. An always-full fruit basket is another healthy and aesthetically pleasing thing to have on your counters. To save space or enhance the look of your kitchen, you could hang your pots and pans on the wall.

Kitchen sink: As the saying goes—"everything but the kitchen sink"—the sink should remain a minimalist's haven! It would help if you kept a small container or a divided tray at the sink to hold a sponge, dishwashing liquid, drain plug, a dish swab to wipe and clean the sink, and a bottle of hand wash. Cluttering your sink will lead to things getting wet, mouldy and unhygienic.

Dishwasher: A solid dishwasher routine and using the appliance effectively can save you a lot of time and money in the long term. It will help you see how many dishes you and your family need and use before it gets full. The packing and unpacking routine can become a little mundane, but it beats standing at the sink when you could spend that time doing something more meaningful.

Stove: Just like your sink, the stuff around your

stove should be kept to a minimum to prevent a build-up of grease and bacteria on these items. Keep a spoon rest or a small plate for the same purpose near your stove to make your cooking easy and convenient. A tall and slim container can be placed near the stove to store at least one cooking spoon, one spatula, and one slotted spoon so that you don't have to consult your drawers at the start of

* * *

Key Takeaways from This Chapter:

In the next chapter, we will tackle how to organize your bathroom to become a place of relaxation and serenity for you and your family. A quick recap of kitchen organization is necessary before we move on.

- The kitchen is the core of the home, and most of the challenges faced when organizing it involves accommodating the various needs of other family members.
- Hygiene, the absence of cluttered spaces, and simplicity are essential in organizing your kitchen.
- The essential zones in a kitchen are the grocery cupboard or pantry; the food preparation area; the refrigerator and freezer area; kitchen cabinets, countertops, kitchen drawers, the sink,

dishwasher, and stove area.

- A two-step ladder, sanitizer, and an erasable board will assist the flow of activity in your kitchen.
- Organizing each zone requires a system prioritizing access to the items you use most often.

* * *

EXERCISE #5

Visualize Your Kitchen Goals

Date:____________

Write down the three areas of your kitchen that you think will be the most challenging to organize. Please close your eyes and visualize how you want these zones to look after you are done organizing them to motivate you to get started.

CHAPTER 6: ORGANIZING YOUR BATHROOM

Simplicity is the ultimate sophistication. –Leonardo da Vinci

A bathroom is an important place in any home. It should ideally be a place of serenity, relaxation, and general *zen*.

Like the kitchen, it is one of the spaces in your home where you start your day by showering, pampering yourself, and getting ready. Executing your morning routine can set the tone for the rest of your day. The bathroom is also a space where we end our day by unwinding after a gruelling schedule. Your bathroom is where you go to be rejuvenated, and it should be organized to bring you a sense of calm.

Similar to your kitchen, you must prioritize cleanliness above all else when deciding how to organize your bathroom. I recommend going the minimalistic route when choosing an organizing system and aesthetic for your bathroom. Clutter in this space leads to dust and bacteria collecting on things and results in a stressful environment where you can't find something you need to access quickly. I chose that particular da Vinci quote above to open this chapter because choosing simplicity will give you the best functionality and aesthetic in your bathroom.

What Are Your Challenges?

Bathrooms, especially in more modern homes, are generally smaller. In some, you can barely stretch your arms out, and the architects and designers have favoured fitting in the essentials over extra comfort. Therefore, space might be your first challenge when tackling your bathroom. The space might already be so tight that once you add in your belongings and products, it becomes even more packed and crowded.

The room's lack of storage space, shelving, and general depth might be another challenge. I've had the experience of opening a bottle full of water because I had to store my shampoo bottle on the shower floor due to the lack of shelving. These challenges are frustrating and can make your bathroom routine seem like another chore on the list. This does not align with the peace, serenity, and rejuvenation goals you should have for your bathroom.

Another challenge might be that you have one bathroom that needs to cater to multiple people of multiple ages.

The members of your household might have different bathroom routines. The experience of waiting your turn during the morning rush as you run late for work, only to arrive in the bathroom and find that the hot water is finished, could be expected. Or, you might have multiple bathrooms that need to be organized according to each user's needs, including a guest bathroom. Unfortunately, I can't tell you how to prevent your teenagers from using up all of the hot water, but I can help you solve the other challenges!

What Do You Need?

The ideal bathroom is a functional and hygienic space where all your essential items are easily accessible and remain clean. The room must be able to be easily cleaned and disinfected regularly.

I urge you to do a deep clean of your bathrooms at least once a week, ideally twice a week. So, you don't want to move too many things around to clean the space properly.

Room for the extra stock is something else you might need to provide when organizing your bathroom. It is a common issue not to have any spare cupboard space to store your extra toilet paper, towels, toiletries, and light bathroom supplies for guests. This means that you have to make the absolute most of your vertical and horizontal space. Therefore, the bathroom is a space where

I would recommend investing in a few affordable and durable storage options.

How you organize your bathroom should complement the room's flow and allow for adequate ventilation throughout the room. Ventilation is essential in a bathroom for hygiene purposes and to prevent mould and humidity from destroying your belongings stored in the room. Therefore, dividing the space into zones will allow you to organize each one correctly. Most bathrooms have the following zones: toilet, bath and shower, sink, hamper or laundry storage area, and cabinets above and under the sink.

What Do You Want?

You need to think carefully about every product you bring into your bathroom. Ask yourself if you need it, and if so, how often you will use it. Anything that can cause unnecessary clutter in your bathroom is something you **want** instead of **needing** there.

Your aesthetic desires for your bathroom also need to be carefully considered. Just picture it—you're in your grandmother's bathroom, and your eyes fall on the seashell ornaments near the sink that haven't been moved, let alone washed for years (maybe decades). Not to mention any grandmas out there, but I recommend that you stay away from unsightly ornaments to keep your bathroom clutter-free, bacteria-free, and within this decade.

Taking Action

The best way to organize your bathroom should be intentional. Select storage solutions that store your valuable or necessary bathroom items in a user-friendly manner. Your bathroom storage solutions should be based on how you live and address the needs of your daily routine. The organizing system you use in your bathroom has to be practical, simple, and effective.

Keep these requirements in mind even if you organize each zone differently. I recommend finding storage containers and devices that match your bathroom to look cohesive and less cluttered.

Remember that you don't have to exhaust your colourful, creative flare in a space that needs to be simple and clean, like the bathroom.

Toilet: Most toilets have ample wall space between the cistern and the window, usually above it.

An aesthetically pleasing and practical storage option for this area is an over-the-toilet ladder. The ladder usually has up to three rungs where you can store a few wicker bins for extra toilet paper, towels, air freshener, and other spare toiletries. You could also divide it so that each family member has their container or basket on this ladder that houses their toiletries. Make sure that the ladder and the bins are easy to clean regularly. Rolling up towels and bathmats is a far more convenient way to store these items. Not only does it look better, but it also makes grabbing one on the go easier than sifting through a pile. You could also invest in narrow shelving next to the toilet or a toilet paper holder that stands up to store excess stock.

Your decisions depend on the layout of your bathroom.

Regarding the toilet itself, please heed my advice and *keep it simple*. Think back to your grandmother's house. In addition to the dusty seashells, she might have also insisted that the toilet be dressed for any occasion by adorning it with one of humanity's most horrific inventions: a toilet lid cover. Please avoid these at all costs, as their only purposes are to collect germs and give you unnecessary and unpleasant items to wash. Place air fresheners, a small succulent plant, or a scented candle on the windowsill to create a fresh atmosphere.

Bath: Your bath is, by definition, a place where you relax and unwind. Affix a stainless-steel hooked rack over the rim for you to hold the essentials such as loofahs, body wash, bath bombs, or scented oils. If you can afford it, use any countertop space on the sides of your bath to place some scented candles or a reed fragrance diffuser to create a relaxing ambience. If you have both a tub and shower in your bathroom, avoid your bath becoming a dumping zone for dirty laundry or a storage zone for spare toiletries.

Shower: This is a goldmine of vertical space. If you're able, install a few narrow glass shelves going up on your shower wall to store your shower essentials like shampoo, conditioner, body wash, soaps, wash cloths, and any other products you use during your shower. Glass shelves will provide the illusion of space, and they're easy to clean. Suppose you can't afford to install shelving. In that case, an inexpensive stainless steel or plastic hanging shower caddy will do the same and make excellent use of the vertical space. If multiple people use one shower, you could give each person a shelf or section of the caddy to store their products.

Sink: This is the prime real estate of the bathroom. The countertop of the sink, if any, should only contain the essentials you use daily. These include a simple glass for your toothbrush and toothpaste and a bottle of hand wash. If you can manage it, install a shelf underneath your bathroom mirror to provide extra storage for other everyday items like mouthwash, dental floss, makeup remover, cotton earbuds, and makeup-removing cotton pads. Be sure to place a trash can near the sink or bathroom. [There should essentially be a trash can in every room in your house to keep things clean and tidy.]

Hamper or Laundry Storage Area: This bathroom area can get particularly untidy, overflow if you don't have a system, and you spend precious time sorting through the dirty laundry before washing it. My solution is simple: invest in two matching slim hampers or laundry baskets. Use one to toss in your white laundry and the other in your colourful laundry.

This saves you time spent separating them before washing. If you don't have the space, or if you live alone, then, of course, use one laundry basket, but the dual solution was life-changing for me, and there are many slim-line and rollable baskets everywhere. I suggest you develop a laundry routine instead of waiting until the basket is full. Doing your laundry at least once a week allows you to assess whether or not you can afford to get rid of a few more items of clothing, depending on what you wear most often.

Cabinets Above the Sink: This is where the non-essentials should go, the stuff you reach for weekly, monthly, or only when you need it. Suppose the cabinet above your sink has a mirror attached. In that case, it is usually relatively shallow, with a few skinny shelves inside. Use this to store medication, serums, face wash, excess toothpaste, mouthwash, dental floss, antiperspirant...anything that is slim enough to fit in. If the cabinet has some depth, use a few mini storage bins or drawer organizers, or repurpose small gift boxes you might have around the house to group different stored items. The groups could be shaving supplies, dental products, skincare products, or any other groups you require. Use the cabinet to keep things you need to see and have easy access to but are not everyday essential bathroom items.

Cabinets Under the Sink: Some bathrooms have this cabinet; others have a sort of open cabinet with shelving but no doors with the sink attached. Organize it by placing the tallest items on the bottom shelf regardless of what you have in your bathroom. These could be spare hand or body wash bottles, shaving cream, shampoo, conditioner, or any detergents you prefer to keep in the bathroom. Group them into categories when placing them in the cabinet or use flat trays to keep them grouped. Next, store spare shaving razors, toothbrushes, skincare products, hair products, and other items you don't use daily on the additional shelves. Keep it organized and tidy by using smaller containers to group items of the exact purpose of the same size—that is up to you. You can also invest in multi-tiered organizers or shelf-risers to create additional storage space in a cabinet without shelves.

A nifty trick is to install hooked racks to hang on the inside of your cabinet doors to store more oversized items like a hairdryer, hair straightener, or an electric barber kit. You can also use this trick on the back of your bathroom door by installing hooks to hang used towels, wash cloths, and bathrobes.

Guest Bathrooms: Your guest bathroom can make or break your guests' experience when visiting your home. Foul odours, dust, and clutter in the guest bathroom can create a negative impression of the rest of your home.

The guest bathroom should be pared down to

contain the complete essentials, leaving room to decorate the room tastefully and create a serene and clean atmosphere.

The essentials for guests are the following: spare toilet paper, a laundry basket, a place to hang their towel, body wash or soap, one shelf in the shower, a glass for their toothbrush and toothpaste, hand wash, a hand towel, and a loofah or washcloth. Scented candles are a must in your guest bathroom. Choose a sophisticated and simple theme for your guest bathroom (seashells, if you must!), but keep it minimal because you want it to be easy to maintain and user-friendly for your guests.

* * *

Key Takeaways from This Chapter

The next chapter will take us into organizing the living room and other "living areas" in your home. Before that, a quick summary of what will make your bathroom the ultimate organized and stress-free zone is necessary.

- When you organize your bathroom, keep the following in mind: "make it about you and how you want others to feel, display what you use, and hide the unnecessary" (Monte, n.d.).
- Avoid unnecessary decorations or other clutter

in your bathroom because it just collects dust and bacteria. A bathroom should be easy to clean regularly.

- The zones in your bathroom must be organized based on your family's everyday needs and routine.
- It is worth investing in extra storage options such as shelving or slim cabinets and organizers that match your bathroom to create a clean look while providing practical solutions.
- Make use of the plentiful vertical space available in every bathroom.
- Most bathrooms have the following zones: toilet, bath and shower, sink, hamper or laundry storage area, and cabinets above and under the sink.
- Make the guest bathroom enjoyable for your guests and also easy to maintain for yourself.
- Keep your bathroom simple, clean and minimal.

* * *

EXERCISE #6

Keep Your Bathroom Alive

Date:____________

Walk through your bathroom and write down five items you have not used in the last three months. Next, clear your countertops in your bathroom by identifying three things you do not reach for daily but still need to keep in the bathroom.

CHAPTER 7: ORGANIZING YOUR LIVING AREAS

Move from having a living room to living with room. –Dalys Macon

The living room and living areas or recreational areas make a house a home. The entire household gathers in this space. They're where you have dinner, watch your favourite show, or celebrate special occasions. The living areas are some of the most used rooms in the home because you spend your downtime and quality time with your partner, pets, and children.

These areas of your home where you can express

your and your family's creative flare. This is the opportunity to show off the eclectic and unique collection of decorative items you kept after successfully decluttering. Organizing these spaces will make you a better host to your guests and ensure that you and your family are comfortable in the areas for relaxation.

What Are Your Challenges?

Your home's living room or recreational spaces might be smaller than required for your family, and there may be limited storage to cater to the multiple functions the areas need. For example, you might need your living to function as a playroom for your children. A major challenge is creating a comfortable and functional space for yourself, your family, your pets, and your guests.

These are also areas that get quickly cluttered because of the activities that occur within them.

Stuff is often left out and not put back, defeating the purpose of relaxation because you spend your time in that space cleaning up instead of enjoying the area. Your challenges might also be that the current organization of the room does not flow most conveniently. The space might also lack character or look too clinical instead of welcoming and cozy.

What Do You Need?

Your home is made up of different living areas with additional needs. Even if your home is small, it is still an excellent strategy to zone out separate spaces for other purposes. These living areas or zones can include the following:

- A living room
- Dining room
- Patio or porch
- The backyard or barbecue area
- The kids' playroom
- The den
- A home office

I've chosen to include tips on organizing your home office in this chapter because it has become a so-called "living area" due to the increasing number of people working from home due to the corporate transformation caused by the COVID-19 pandemic. Like the bathroom, living areas are spaces where I would recommend investing in some space-saving storage options because the things used in these spaces need to be put away when they're not used to avoid them creating clutter and causing you stress as you go about your daily routine.

What Do You Want?

From my experience, the most common request when organizing living areas in a home is that people want them to be stylish yet warm and inviting. This is sometimes a tall order, but if you follow my practical tips, prioritize precisely what you need to access, and create a routine to ensure the items used in these spaces are put away after use, you can achieve your desired aesthetic in these spaces.

Keeping these spaces clutter-free and organized means you can effortlessly host that game night, play date, or dinner party that you have been avoiding. More importantly, you're able to transform the time spent in these spaces into quality time with your family or friends by having everything you need at hand to enjoy family movie night, a lazy night alone, or a romantic evening with your partner.

<u>Taking Action</u>

As we move through organizing each space, remember that your organizing system must be tailored to work for your family and lifestyle, especially in these living areas. Cumbersome gadgets or inconvenient methods to access things or put them away will lead you back to stress and clutter in these spaces. Think about the natural order in which you would do something, move around the room, and reach for things.

<u>Living Room:</u> First, plan your living room correctly based on your pathway to the kitchen and other house rooms. The last thing you want is moving a sofa back and forth to pass through constantly. The best way to maximize the space you have in your living room is to invest in furniture that also serves as storage. Go for a vintage aesthetic by placing a classic-looking trunk in the center of the living room to serve as a coffee table and a storage option. Alternately, you can choose from various classy coffee tables with shelving, drawers, and sealable storage space to provide two essential functions in your living room. You can place your extra blankets, cushions, board games, kids' toys (if you don't have a separate playroom), or you are even reading material within this storage space. Your television stand can also provide additional storage space to store gaming consoles, DVDs, and CDs. Seating with storage space-like sealable ottomans is another excellent option.

If you have a small living room, I suggest using vertical storage space, which can also serve as decor. So, erect a storage ladder, a bookshelf, floating shelves, or a durable wall rack instead of using an entire wall for a large painting or mirror. This way, you can decorate the room and store items like books, DVDs, and sentimental items on the shelving. Use a stylish tray to give your remotes a home and keep them together. A side table or two can increase your storage space if they have shelving or drawers. Use cord organizers, cable ties, or trunking to hide the cords of your plugged-in devices. This will also prevent dust build-up.

Maintaining the organizing system in your living room means acknowledging that it is a space that will continuously accumulate clutter. Acknowledge this and find a solution. A possible explanation is a clutter bin that you empty at least once a week to put everything in it back where it belongs. You could also work five to ten minutes into your daily home cleaning routine to tidy up everything in the living room. Taking five minutes to move around the room, and picking up any clutter, will save you time in the long term and keep you, and not the chaos, in control of the room.

Dining Room: Vertical storage is your friend in your dining room. Effective use of vertical space aids the room's flow and ensures that you have enough storage and room to avoid your guests feeling cramped while eating.

A simple credenza, sideboard, vintage buffet, or a sophisticated server can transform your dining room into the ultimate eating venue because you will be able to store all the cutlery, crockery, linen, and glassware required for that space conveniently. If you have the space, you could also create a bar area in your dining room. Glassware and a few bottles of alcohol create a unique aesthetic and conversation piece while serving the purpose of storing these items. When organizing your bar, group the same types of alcohol.

For example, display your collection of gins, white wines, red wines, whiskeys, or vodkas by storing them together. The same applies to glassware. Store your gin glasses, shot glasses, and wine glasses separately so that you're not searching for a drink instead of spending time with your guests.

If you don't have the space to place additional furniture in your dining room, or if you have an open-plan dining room linked to your kitchen then I recommend storing your dining room items in your kitchen. Hence, they're within reach when you need them. Aim always to keep the dining room table clear. I've noticed that for families who usually have their meals in the living room, the dining room tends to become the "junk drawer" for work and school documents, unfolded laundry, and grocery items you intend to pack away. Be strict about this and keep this space is clear.

Patio/Porch: This space is often where you would spend time unwinding with a cocktail or entertaining guests. Keep it minimalistic by keeping only the essentials you need here. I would recommend investing in some durable and weather-proof outdoor furniture that is also easy to clean for this space. You want to avoid cleaning up chairs and tables when your guests arrive.

Backyard/ Barbecue Area: Once again, durable outdoor furniture is the way to go. If you can afford the space, create a mini dining room and kitchen organization system near your grill. Keep your picnic cutlery, crockery, and glassware in a weather-proof storage bin or sealable shelving outside with the grill. Solo cups, paper plates, and plastic knives and forks also work great for an outdoor space. You don't have to make an elaborate garden party from a scene of *Bridgerton* your entertaining standard if you and your family prepare a more casual style.

Kids' Playroom: Your kids' toys can be a massive undertaking to organize. Your kids might be reluctant to part with their favourite teddy bear (that now has half an eye and three-quarters of an ear left), or they might not want to learn how to clean up after themselves because they see it as a necessary chore. If your kids' toys stay in your living room, create a zone for them, and use colourful cubbies and storage bins to store their toys, books, and games. Another option is to get them to help you decorate a few boxes to use as toy storage. This gives them ownership of their organized space and will motivate them to want to put their toys back into *their* box.

Minimalism blogger, Ema Hidlebaugh, describes a concept called "toy rotation," where you only keep a certain number of toys out at a time. Then you change these out for a new bunch of toys after a week or a month (Hidlebaugh, 2021). This system mainly works for toddlers because the toys in the new rotation feel like new toys to them. The benefits of using the design are the following: "less clutter and stress, more independent and creative play for your child, more time to play and less time spent on tidying up, and it is easier to tidy up than a mountain of toys, of which they only play with ten" (Hidlebaugh, 2021).

If you have a separate playroom for your children, make the space fun, creative, and inviting by using colour, murals, and pictures of their favourite movie or television show characters. Create zones in the playroom for reading, painting, playing, and doing schoolwork, and organize these areas in a way that makes keeping the playroom organized almost like a game for them. Giving your children their play zone or room will teach them good organizing habits and help them get into a routine of putting things back where they belong after using them. You must involve the other members in your household—especially your children—in your organizing routine so that it is manageable and can be done even if you're not home.

Den: A den can be a genuinely creative space because you can include an eclectic and diverse range of items that reflect your or your family's interests and hobbies. The den can be adorned with movie posters, pop culture memorabilia, items that are sentimental to you, a record player, board games, a pool table—basically any variety of things you want to include. Make comfort and creativity your priorities when organizing this space instead of strictly managing for tidiness. Make it a project that you complete over time because this is another space that should remain warm and inviting. Avoid clutter by placing a trash can in this room and, like in your living room, spend five minutes daily walking through the room and putting things back where they belong.

Home Office: Working from home has become the norm for many people since the COVID-19 pandemic forced us to spend months inside our homes. Your home office should be a tranquil, neat, and clean space where you can focus on your tasks and work. I prefer an office with a clear desk containing a few helpful storage pieces, like a small desk organizer with slots for pens and post-it notes. A quirky or plain mug is a great way to store your pens, pencils, and highlighters on your desk. The type of desk you have determines how cluttered your desk will become. Find a desk with a matching cabinet that slides underneath, or invest in a storage trolley to store spare stationery, paper, and your electronic devices. Use cord bundlers or cord zippers to keep cords together. Paper can quickly become a clutter hazard, and it is something we all use, receive, and need daily. Keep a paper tray or box on your desk for the most urgent files. I recommend the filing system below to organize, prioritize, and store your papers. You can use actual files, a concertina file, separate colour-coded folders, or a filing cabinet to store these, depending on your spatial limits.

1. Action papers: This can be a bin or basket containing bills that must be paid and other important documents that require you to do something. Receipts or coupons shouldn't be kept in this category.
2. Reference papers: This can include food or product catalogues that you want to order from later; cards for services that you might use in future; or manuals for your appliances.
3. Short-term papers: This contains invoices or receipts for items you have recently purchased and might need to return. The papers in this category must be kept only temporarily.
4. Long-term papers: Documents relating to taxes, contracts, mortgage papers, medical, and insurance policies.
5. Memory papers: Here, you would organize and store photos, awards, letters, certificates, and other sentimental paper items.

* * *

Key Takeaways from This Chapter

We will be taking on the challenge of organizing your bedroom and closet in the next chapter, so let us recap the main ways to achieve peace of mind in your living areas before we move on.

- Living areas in your home include a living room, dining room, patio or porch, the backyard or barbecue area, the kids' playroom, the den, and a home office.
- Acknowledging that these spaces are bound to accumulate clutter daily will help you decide on an organizing routine.
- Spending five minutes picking up stuff you have used in these spaces, and putting them back where they belong, is enough to keep them organized.
- Warm and inviting should be the goals when organizing living spaces, as opposed to rigid and clinical.
- Celebrate the decorative and sentimental items you kept after decluttering to bring these spaces to life and make them unique to your home.
- Investing in furniture that dually functions as storage is the key to success in organizing living areas.

* * *

EXERCISE #7

Rotate and Appreciate

Date:___________

Identify the top ten toys your child plays with regularly and make these the first in this month's toy rotation schedule. Write down three things about your living room space that you like, or find attractive, to motivate you to organize it. Get rid of at least five scattered papers around your home office before organizing this space.

CHAPTER 8: ORGANIZING YOUR BEDROOM AND CLOSET

If you go anywhere, even paradise, you will miss your home. –Malala Yousafzai

The condition of your bedroom and closet directly affects your mental health by raising or lowering your stress levels. Statistics show that "approximately 80% of most medical spending is stress-related compared to other issues" (Peysakhovich, 2022). Your bedroom is the first room you see when you open your eyes and

the last before getting that all-important rest so you can function at your best during the day. Because of the importance of these spaces, how you organize them can determine whether you have a great day or a terrible one.
What Are Your Challenges?

Studies show that "57% of women have said that they have issues organizing their closets. This has added to their overall stress levels when trying to find things they need from their closets in a hurry" (Peysakhovich, 2022). Your morning routine might be challenging enough given the limited time you have to get ready for work; your disorganized clothes and cosmetics add to this challenge. Not being able to find clothes or other items you're looking for can cause significant frustration and result in you being grumpy for the rest of the day. Other possible challenges are space, storage, and not knowing where to start categorizing your clothes.

What Do You Need?

Your bedroom must set you up for a successful day or a peaceful night. You need to wake up feeling refreshed instead of stressed and go to sleep feeling relaxed instead of thinking about the million things you need to do. Your room needs to be comfortable and functional, contain your essentials, and represent you. Your closet requires to function in the way that works best for you. You might wear a uniform to work, work out at the gym, or work from home and want to make the most of your social life.

The zones, organizing system, and closet maintenance must be viable for you not to be burdened.

What Do You Want?

You may want to store your linen in your bedroom for further convenience or organize your room so you can get dressed instead of in the bathroom. Spaces for your jewelry, cosmetics, hair products, fragrances, and accessories might be further goals you have for your bedroom.

Completing a workout or yoga routine before you leave your room in the mornings might be another desirable goal for your bedroom. Working in a reading nook is another common request when organizing a bedroom. This can be a very tranquil space but be wary of cluttering the chair or sitting in the reading nook with random clothes or other items. When determining your organizing goals for your closet, remember to continually assess the room and what you could use around the house before buying new storage products.

Taking Action When Organizing Your Bedroom

Bed Area

Your nightstands or side tables that flank either side of your bed are important pieces of furniture because they contain the essential items you require for your morning and evening routine. These essentials often include your phone, charger, watch, medication, water bottle, that book you just can't put down, bedside lamp, glasses, hand cream, and lip balm. If your nightstands have shelves or drawers, make the best use of those spaces by using them as additional storage, but be careful not to clutter them with random papers, electronic devices, and work files that cause stress. The space under your bed can be used as additional storage if your space is minimal, and it will require regular cleaning because of the possibility of dust building up.

When it comes to your bed, it depends on your personal preference. You might be someone who loves to have plenty of throw cushions on your bed, or you might be more minimalistic and prefer a bare mattress. Whatever your tastes, making your bed every day is an excellent way to start your day off on a positive note. It prepares you for the day, and coming home to the sight of an unmade bed can stress you out later. Don't worry about recreating a hotel turndown when you make your bed; make sure to give your sheets and pillows a good shake and that it at least looks neat.

Investing in a good-quality headboard will lift the room and complete the aesthetic of your bed. Your headboard can match the design of your room, or it can serve as a standout piece in the room. Use a linen spray on your sheets when making your bed daily. This keeps your mattress smelling fresh and might reduce how often you need to change your sheets. I recommend changing them once a month or once weekly if you have pets that cuddle up on your bed.

Linen

Ideally, please store your linen near your bed. A sophisticated-looking trunk or storage kist placed at the foot of your mattress is an excellent way to keep your linen if you have the space for it. If there is no space near your bed, dedicate at least one or half of a closet to linen.

My advice is that you shouldn't buy excessive amounts of linen because, even though having a variety is excellent, they take up a lot of storage space. Between five to eight good quality sets of linen is more than enough. Store them in their locations by folding everything into a square, slipping the matching pillowcases and fitted sheet between the folded duvet cover to keep them together, and searching for a fitted sheet that is stored separately from its matching pillowcase covers wastes precious time.

Arrange your linen closet or chest according to colour so the sets look like the spines of books you can select and quickly pull out. By this, I mean avoid stacking them on top of each other. The bookshelf method looks better than a pile and takes up less space if the linen is folded correctly.

Incidentally, folding a fitted sheet often baffles people, and it is easier than you think. Lay the sheet so the edges that crease and fold over face you. Fold in the long sides until it becomes a rectangle. Fold the length of the rectangle into thirds. Lastly, fold this length into a square.

Dressing Area

The functionality of your dressing room or area can set the tone of your day because this is where you spend time getting ready and gathering your thoughts for the day ahead. Your dresser contains more prime real estate than you realize. Simply putting in some mini storage bins, baskets, repurposed boxes or box lids, or drawer organizers can transform these drawers or cabinets into your very own beauty bar.

Makeup: When organizing makeup and cosmetics,

you have a few options for managing systems. You can choose to organize these by brand, by the type of product they are (e.g. lipsticks, powders, or eyeliners), by colour, or in sets of how often you use them. For example, you might have five products you use daily as makeup for work and other products reserved for special occasions. You can store these products upright with the label up to identify them or lie down so you can see the colour if you have the space.

Jewelry: These are often sentimental and valuable items; therefore, how you organize and store them needs to be respected. Clear compartment organizers are the best way to organize your precious jewels, watches, and other accessories. Categorize them by their type and what they're made of, or store them in sets if you have necklaces with matching rings and earrings.

Fragrances: Perfumes are often almost as valuable as jewelry and are always used in moderation to last a long time. Therefore, you must store them in a way that makes this possible. The most stable form of storing fragrances is upright and in some containers or trays away from direct sunlight or heat, so they don't evaporate. A mirrored tray with handles, or a substantial lip around the edge, has worked best for me personally. These also come in two-tiered options if you have many perfumes to store.

Your dresser is also home to other items such as hairbrushes, curlers, hair straighteners, hair dryers, nail products, body products, hair ties, grooming tools, and many more. Categorize these items, and then organize them further within their category so that you save time when looking for them. For example, a hairbrush would be its category. Then combs, round brushes, and wet hairbrushes would be sub-categories within the larger one.

Taking Action When Organizing Your Closet

The closet is a necessary space for everyone. Still, it also causes the most stress regarding home management. The problem is that you organize it once. Then nothing seems to be able to fit back where it went, or you no longer have time to maintain the organizational system.

Your closet needs to be organized according to priority, clothing categories, functionality, and accessibility. An organized closet will always be visually appealing regardless of the method used. Imagine a clothing store and make that your organizing ideal.

When you're ready to start, haul everything out onto your bed, and start sorting your clothes. The key with clothes is to organize them by clothing type and then further organize that type by colour, brand, what you use them for, or how often you use them. You can create your system by categorizing your work clothes and casual clothes into their groups and then organizing them within these groupings by colour.

Deciding what goes where can be challenging, and you can spend lots of time changing things around until you find the perfect balance. Considering shelving in your closet, consider investing in clear storage bins to store categories together. Labelling the containers makes access even more effortless. If you have a lot of drawer space, keep the bins to a minimum. Suitable quality hangers will also preserve the quality of your clothes over time. You must be able to see everything when you open your closet, and the clothes stored out of sight remain unused and eventually become clutter. Think about your routine and prioritize what you naturally reach for in your closet and the order you get for these items. The categories and ways to organize them described below will hopefully inspire you to adapt your wardrobe using this type of system.

Underwear: Small yet critical, your underwear deserves a prime spot in your closet. A few clear and shallow bins or drawers will suffice to store these. Fold the bottom up, and then fold the length into thirds to create a square.

Organize them according to colour and store them vertically with the fold facing upwards instead of horizontally piling them on top of each other. This ensures you can see everything and, more importantly, *use* everything.

Socks: We've seemingly been conditioned to roll our socks into each other and store them as oddly shaped bundles that take up a lot of space. Save space and increase the life of the elastic on your socks by placing one sock on top of the other and simply folding the pair in half. Organize them first by length and then by colour. Store them vertically with the fold facing upwards in a clear bin or drawer. You will be amazed at how much space you save and how visually awesome this looks!

Scarves, Belts and Ties: I've combined these two items simply because they can be hung. Create space by installing hooks or a thin rack inside your closet doors to turn these items. Organize them by colour so you can quickly grab these accessories to match any outfit. Scarves and ties can also be neatly rolled up, sorted by colour, and stored in clear bins or drawers if you prefer.

Sleepwear: I recommend storing all sleepwear in either storage bins or drawers. Separate your belongings into summer and winter sleepwear and keep them in readymade pairs that you can grab and go. This means storing a pair of boxer shorts and a shirt together as a set. Fold the

items into squares and place them together to save storage space. Pack them vertically with the fold facing upwards, giving you a complete view of everything in that category.
Fold your long and short sleeve T-shirts, jackets, and hoodies, by smoothing the shirt out with the front facing up. Fold each side of the shirt into the middle to create a rectangle. Fold the shirt into thirds from top to bottom, then fold this rectangle in half.

Gym Clothes: These can also be stored as sets in their separate section, drawer, or storage bin. Keeping a pre-packed gym bag in your car or closet that you replenish after each trip to the gym is a smart way to ensure that you use and rotate all of your gym clothes while saving you the time spent rummaging for that pair of cycling shorts. Store your gym clothes and gym towels together for further convenience.

T-shirts: These can either be folded and stored vertically per the folding method described for sleepwear, or they can be hung up, depending on your closet space. Be wary of the shoulders of your T-shirts getting stretched out if you hang them up. You may be forced to hang them up if you don't have the drawer or shelf space to fold them. Arrange them by colour, and make sure to further separate the different types of T-shirts within the T-shirt category, like long-sleeve, short-sleeve, golfers, and polos.

Pants and Jeans: Create an actual home-shopping experience by organizing your pants by type, then by colour. Jeans can be placed into their separate section, like the denim bar in a clothing shop. Organize your jeans by their shade, and either hang them or store them vertically in bins or baskets on shelves or in drawers.

Your pants, jeans, and shorts can also be folded into neat squares by spreading the pants out on a surface and folding one leg over the other with the crotch facing. Fold the crotch in so that a straight line is formed. Fold the pants into thirds from top to bottom and stand them upright to be packed vertically.

Swimwear: This should be stored in sets as a separate category and categorized by colour. Choose where to keep your swimwear based on how often you use it. If you reach for it once a year, store it in a part of your closet that you hardly see.

Coats, Sweaters, and Jackets: Coats and jackets should ideally be hung up and take up too much space if folded into drawers or storage bins. If you don't have the freedom to hang them up, fold them into tight squares, and store them vertically. They should be sorted according to their heaviness, meaning heavy winter coats will be at one end and light jackets at the other and then arranged by colour within these categories. I advise folding your fleece or woollen sweaters because hanging them up can make them stretch and lose their shape.

Dresses: These should be hung up and organized by colour. You can further categorize dresses by separating those you wear casually from those you wear for work and then organize these by colour.

Formal Wear: Suits can be hung up assets in their section or separated into jackets, shirts and pants, then arranged by colour. Keep your ties nearby if you wear suits regularly because you want easy access to the entire outfit.

Sunglasses: These can be sorted by brand, colour, shape, or how often you use them. They can have their separate shelf where you stack them, one behind the other, going from the back to the front of the frame. You could also install a vertical storage option on the wall near your closet or dresser, with compartments to store each pair.

Hats and Caps: For some, these are collector's items and highly valued. If you're a hat or cap collector, install shelving or a display case to showcase your collection. If you're just a casual user of these items, store them in a hat box or on hooks inside your closet door. Hats and caps can be arranged by colour or by brand.

Handbags and Bags: Arrange these by colour or brand and store them higher up in your closet on shelving, in clear storage bins, or baskets. Make sure you can see your bags
so you're inspired to rotate them and use them properly.

Shoes: Some people are lucky enough to have a separate closet for shoes to create unique displays of their impressive collections of sneakers or high heels. Most of us have to use the floor space in our cabinets to store our shoes. Start by arranging your shoes by their type. Types include sneakers, sandals, boots, formal shoes, high heels, slip-on, trainers, and slippers. Next, organize the different varieties of each type. For example, you could have ankle boots, thigh-high boots, and combat boots. Finally, organize these varieties according to either height, colour, or brand. Shelf risers, shoe racks, and storage bins or baskets are great solutions to create extra storage.

High Storage Areas: Use the very top shelves of your closet to store items you use on rare occasions. These include suitcases, traditional wear arranged by colour, ball gowns, and Halloween costumes. The top shelves can also store spare linen, pillows, and heavy blankets.

* * *

Key Takeaways from This Chapter

The spaces we will focus on in the next chapter are the garage, attic, and basement. Let's recap to ensure your closet will never stress you out again.

- Your bedroom and closet can be the most stress-inducing spaces if they're disorganized.
- The bedroom comprises the bed zone, dressing zone, and linen zone, and the organization of these zones depends on your routine.
- Restrict your bedroom to the essentials to ensure it stays clutter-free.
- You should model your closet after a clothing store to get it organized.
- The following are the most important categories within your closet: underwear, socks, scarves, belts, ties, sleepwear, gym clothes, T-shirts, pants, jeans, swimwear, coats, sweaters, jackets, dresses, formal wear, sunglasses, hats, caps, handbags, bags, shoes, and high storage areas.
- Separate your items into their categories, organize them by sub-categorizing them into smaller groups, if required, and finally arrange them by colour or brand.

* * *

EXERCISE #8

The Everyday Essentials

Date:___________

Write down three essential items you need at your bedside or nightstand. Think about how you decide what to wear in the morning. Do you choose your shoes, shirt, or bottoms first? Use this to help you zone out of your closet.

CHAPTER 9: ORGANIZING YOUR GARAGE, BASEMENT, AND ATTIC

Let go of things you don't love; find homes for things you do. –Ema Hidlebaugh

The spaces we will organize in this chapter are often chosen as the backdrop for some of the scariest scenes in many horror movies. Everyday use of the trope is when the main character heads into the basement, garage, or attic to search for an escape route, only to be confronted by the menacing villain. A struggle usually ensues, and the suspense leaves you never knowing who will survive right until the end. You might be the person heading into your garage, basement, or attic to confront a villain you know all too well: those scattered Christmas decorations, miscellaneous documents, or those power tools you've left lying around.

The three spaces at the heart of this chapter are often spaces we avoid because we don't need access to their contents every day. It's ok to admit that you've ignored your garage until the time arrived last year to haul out those Halloween decorations. For these spaces, it's not about the items stored but *how* they're stored. Typical items in these spaces include holiday decorations, random documents, tools, garden equipment, old toys, pool-related supplies, camping equipment, sports equipment, outdoor furniture, emergency kits, and musical instruments.

What Are Your Challenges?

Ignoring these three spaces can weigh quite heavily on your mind and affect how proud you feel about the actual level of organization of your household. Organizing these rooms is usually the final step in cementing that sense of achievement and completeness that you have finally managed your entire home. Depending on the location of your home, the natural condition of these rooms is usually challenging to control, so they're exposed to fluctuating temperatures, dust, humidity, mould, and mildew. Therefore, potential damage to your belongings in these spaces is a common challenge. Another challenge is that these areas have become dumping grounds for stuff you intend to organize later, sell, or donate. Putting off enjoying your hobbies, your favourite sports, swimming, or a camping trip could result from disorganized rooms because you can either never find what you're looking for, or you get so overwhelmed at the mountain of stuff to sift through that you give up. Your main obstacle to getting the space organized is because you have limited space. After all, you only have a garage, attic, or basement, and you can't see a way to get everything in order.

What Do You Need?

You need access to your essential or seasonal items without the risk of an avalanche of boxes, papers, and Christmas baubles attacking you. Your organizing system needs to prioritize the most frequently used stuff. Because you need to protect your belongings from dust, mould, and mildew damage, you need to store them in the most air-tight way possible. Once you assess the space, you might want to invest in clear storage bins or any other durable and sealable storage option that you can also clearly label to know exactly what is stored where. Being able to park a car or two in your garage might also be necessary, and you have to organize the stuff around the space taken up by the vehicles.

If you have a garage, basement, attic, or any combination of these, you will need to decide what to store in each room depending on how the temperature will affect the stuff stored in the room. You need to zone out the space, regardless of how cramped it may seem. If you have a clear idea of where you want to store each category, you will make the best use of your space. Finally, you might need to further declutter these spaces by being deliberate and thinking about what you need, instead of what you're unnecessarily keeping.

What Do You Want?

Take a moment to visualize what you want your garage, basement, or attic to look like. I doubt you're imagining the spine-chilling final scene of the terrifying horror movie, complete with a creepy doll lying in your attic. I would imagine it's more like the shelves of your favourite hardware store or sporting goods store, and this is a great idea to have in mind as you start to categorize your stuff. You essentially want these spaces to function as organized storage for the excess and bulky stuff that can't be stored in the everyday areas of your home so that your daily, weekly, and monthly organizing routine runs smoothly without you having to vacuum around a mountain bike placed in the middle of the dining room.

In terms of your garage, you might also want it to function as a creative space where you can paint, draw, play games like table tennis, foosball, or pool, or where complete woodwork and other craft projects. Be sure not to forget your hobbies when organizing your garage because this makes your home unique and allows you to enjoy your home truly.

As a caution, I recommend that you don't store the following items in your garage, basement, or attic unless they're sealed correctly in air-tight and waterproof containers to avoid them being damaged: chemicals, flammable liquids, delicate fabrics, valuable artwork, food items, photographs, documents, and wooden items.

<u>Taking Action</u>

Garage

This is the most common space in most modern homes out of the three areas we tackle in this

chapter. Remember that the items I recommend that you store in your basement and attic can also be safely stored in the garage by following my practical tips if you only have a garage.
Start by telling yourself that you will topple the ceiling-high mountain of boxes staring back at you by organizing it into submission, and it will not conquer you. After motivating yourself, estimate the space you will need to park your car(s) in the garage comfortably. By 'comfortably,' I mean you must be able to fully open your car doors without denting it into a surfboard or lawnmower as you arrive home from a long day. Don't look at the space used to park the cars; instead, look at it as space you have created to improve your life by decluttering and getting organized.

Next, zone out your garage. You will likely need sections for the following categories: tools, sports equipment, gardening equipment, camping, outdoor shoes, gym bags, emergency items, and musical instruments.

Items in your garage are usually large, bulky, and sometimes even dangerous, so it's not always easy to group and organize them by colour and display them. They need to be categorized based on their use and size. Consider this when you decide how to store them to make sure you make the best use of the valuable vertical storage space in your garage. Keeping a ladder in your garage is non-negotiable, as it ensures your safety and forces you to keep things organized because you can put things back where they belong.

Install shelving or some sturdy racks along your garage walls and invest in ample and clear storage bins to store each category of stuff. Taking the time to label each container is life-changing and will make you perfect your organizing system even further. The garage is where you can store space up to the ceiling because you usually don't reach for these items daily or even once a year.

Tools: Tools must be stored together with their fittings. For example, your power drill should be held with its fittings, bits, nails, and screws so that you have access to everything you need to use it. Mount hammers, pliers, and saws on the walls, to prevent injuring yourself while rummaging through drawers searching for them.

Sports Equipment: Mount your large items like skis, bicycles, surfboards, baseball bats, and hockey sticks on the wall to create an aesthetic that also displays your interests. Footballs, baseballs, and basketballs can be stored in storage bins or wire baskets.

Gardening Equipment: Mount your shears, clippers, and shovels on the wall to save horizontal space. Make sure to store planter pots, watering cans, gardening gloves, and garden ornaments near these wall-mounted items so that the category and zone remain intact. Using a solid wall hook to mount your lawnmower is a game-changer that makes the room look much less cluttered.

Musical Instruments: If you can afford the space, place your drum kit on a mat that can easily slide in and out of the garage. Mount guitars, saxophones, and keyboards on the wall to create your music store. These valuable items should be respected and displayed when they're not used.

Camping Equipment: Your flashlights, folded tents, sleeping bags, outdoor cooking equipment, batteries, and flare guns should all be stored in labelled storage containers in their separate subcategories. It is vital with this category to replenish essential survival items if you used them up on a previous trip. Bug spray, bottled water, batteries, and cooking gas must be fully topped, or in complete working order before you go on your next trip.

Emergency Items: These kits often include bottled water, flashlights, protein bars, blankets, a fire extinguisher, and canned foods. Store them in labelled storage containers and separate the items into each subcategory. Your emergency kit should be stored in an easily accessible location in your garage.

Outdoor Shoes and Bags: Install shelving or use a

shelf riser next to the door connecting your main house to your garage to store outdoor shoes to keep the mud out of your home. You can also store your pre-packed gym or school bag by using adhesive hooks on the wall next to this door to make your mornings flow smoothly.

Basement

Your basement is most likely where pesky mould and mildew will settle, so you should ensure that anything you store in this space is off the ground and stored in air-tight, waterproof containers. Not being able to control the temperature of your basement means you must consider carefully what items you want to keep here. I recommend installing shelving or racks and investing in good quality and tight storage containers. Shelving or racks, make sure you utilize most of the vertical space while leaving the basement floor clear. Place a large plastic table in the middle of your basement to create additional storage space or even a workspace for craft projects that you don't want to overtake your living room or dining room table.

I recommend storing durable outdoor furniture—like plastic chairs and tables—in your basement. Your children's favourite toys, which are no longer being used daily, that you'd like to pass on as family heirlooms, can also be stored in the basement in storage bins. Important documents or document archives can be held here for easy access. Still, they must be organized according to my document priority method in Chapter 7, filed, and stored in waterproof containers. Extra cans of paint, roof tiles, ceramic tiles, and other items you might need to do touch-ups in your home can be stored in the basement. Your spare detergents and non-perishable foods can also be stored on shelves above ground in the basement so you can easily access them in your home. Remember your system of grouping items in the same category and then organizing them into subcategories when arranging them.

In some homes, the washing machine and dryer are set up in the basement. If this is the case in your home, store all items required to do your laundry on shelving above the washing machine and dryer. These items include washing powder or liquid, fabric softener, bleach, and laundry baskets to carry your laundry to and from the basement. Don't store stuff on top of the machines, because this will damage them and is also dangerous.

Attic

It is well-established that attics are cramped with almost no vertical space for shelving, and it is common for the dust to accumulate here. Even though the loft is sometimes better ventilated and less humid than your basement, temperature changes can still cause damage to your belongings, so, just like the garage and the basement, carefully think about what you store here and how often you will need access to those items. Start by zoning your attic by dividing it in half into two distinct zones: holiday decorations in one zone and everything else in the other.

The most common items stored in the attic are holiday decorations, including Christmas, Halloween, and birthday decorations. These items can be challenging to categorize and contain without a system. Categorize your decorations by the holiday they relate to, and Christmas decorations should be separated from Halloween decorations.

Next, sort them by type, meaning group all tinsels together, all baubles together, and all Christmas tree ornaments together. Lastly, and only if applicable, organize them by colour. Use clear storage bins or repurposed boxes to store the items, and make sure to clearly label them so you can quickly identify them when the holidays come around again.

Now that you successfully conquered those holiday decorations, tackle the "everything else" zone in your attic. Use this space to store essential documents, suitcases, extra linen, or extra mattresses. Records and linen must be kept in air-tight containers, and mattresses stored in the attic must be wrapped to prevent intensive dust damage.

* * *

Key Takeaways from This Chapter

Organizing your special sentimental items is the next category we will explore. Before we move on, let's recap the tips we've covered for getting your garage, basement, and attic into good shape before the holidays or your annual camping trip arrives.

- You've been avoiding organizing these spaces because you hardly use the stuff in them. Successfully organizing them can make you feel in control of the organization of your entire home.
- These three areas are prone to mould, dust, and mildew accumulation that damages your stuff, so you have to think carefully about your storage and organizing system.
- Don't store chemicals, flammable liquids, delicate fabrics, valuable artwork, food items, photographs, documents, and wooden items in these rooms unless they're sealed correctly in air-tight and waterproof containers to avoid them being damaged.
- Make use of vertical space where you can.

Investing in clear storage bins, installing shelving, wall-mounting large and hazardous items, and labelling everything will set you up for success in these spaces.

- Store the following in your garage: tools, sports equipment, gardening equipment, musical instruments, camping equipment, emergency items, and outdoor shoes and bags.
- Store the following in your basement: outdoor furniture, kids' toys that are no longer in use, archived documents, extra paint, detergents, and perishable foods.
- Store the following in your attic: holiday decorations, documents, extra linen, and extra mattresses.

* * *

EXERCISE #9

Highest Priority Gets Easiest Access

Date:___________

Write down ten items or categories of things you want to store in your garage, basement, or attic. Next to each item or type, write down how often you use or need the item. Rank the things from what you use the most to what you use the least. Store the highest-ranking item in the garage.

CHAPTER 10: ORGANIZING SENTIMENTAL ITEMS

Happiness is not having what you want. It is wanting what you have. – Rabbi Hyman Judah Schachtel

Hopefully, you have made it through the processes described in my first two books in this series and have decluttered your home and mind. While doing so, you would have made tough decisions about the sentimental items you wanted to keep and those you got rid of. Sentimental items can include photographs, clothing, journals, letters, artwork, memorabilia, ornaments, toys, cards, books, concert tickets and collectors' items like comics, action figures, or model cars. These items might invoke special memories and feelings of a specific period in your life or remind you of a dearly departed loved one.

Your decision to keep these items might have been tough, leaving the things in a state of organizing limbo of them either being helpful, being displayed, being packed away, or becoming dust collectors. It is best to deal with items at the end of your organizing journey so that you can take the time you need to decide how you want to cherish and respect your sentimental items.

Sentimental items often represent our past and positive periods in our lives that we want to reflect on. Acknowledging or commemorating our history is essential because it reminds us of our goals and of how we've progressed. However, be wary of clinging onto the physical belongings from your past in a way that prevents you from moving forward.

What Are Your Challenges?

Organizing sentimental items can be challenging for some of us because of the emotions these items bring up. These complicated feelings are ordinary and extremely common, so don't despair if you dread organizing these items. You might regret letting go of certain items while keeping others. You're stressing out because you believe that getting rid of the item equates to losing the memory associated with the object. The idea of these items not being somewhere in your house makes you feel sad, stressed, or guilty towards the person or period they relate to. The items might keep you anchored to that person or time and you're struggling to either store them away or display them.

Then, the items you have kept might be challenging to categorize, arrange, display, or store. Your concerns might be that your sentimental items are too diverse to be held in one place in your home. The other extreme of this challenge is that because you're reluctant to let them go, your sentimental items might be slowly transforming into clutter, taking over spaces in your home that you need to be cleared for daily use, and seeing them burdens you mentally.

What Do You Need?

Almost every challenge relating to sentimental items raised in the above paragraph can be solved by properly assessing your organizational needs in terms of these items. If you regret what you got rid of, you must pause and reflect. Focus on what you kept instead because these are things that, based on your instinct, were more important or valuable to you. As per my other two books in this series, you need to adopt a progressive or forward-thinking mindset to succeed at home management. You should be proud of the difficult decisions you made when you chose what to keep during the decluttering process.

Organizing the sentimental items you decided to keep means you need to think about how a thing makes you feel and how you would like to respect, protect, and make the most of it. If the number of sentimental items you have kept is starting to stress you out, consider doing more decluttering in this category. If your things are challenging to categorize, remember that they don't all have to be displayed or stored together; you can create a system that works for you.

The most important rule to remember when dealing with sentimental items is that the memory or emotion connected to the item is actually what you're attached to, not the object itself. The memory is what you should cherish because these memories can never be taken away from you.

What Do You Want?

Sentimental items can often represent our creative

sides, so your design goals and vision are essential to sort through these items. You might want to display your sentimental items in a display case, or on shelves, in a dedicated area of your home. These items are often conversation pieces for your guests if they're displayed in a neat and organized way.

You might want to keep every piece in a collection because it is essential for you or it is financially valuable. This goal would apply to collectors' items like vintage comic books, artwork, models, and action figures. Your goal might be eventually to pass these items on to your children or to insure them. This means they must be stored or displayed to remain in mint condition and not get damaged.

Seeing your items daily might be another organization goal for your sentimental stuff. You might want to be able to look through them conveniently whenever you want those nostalgic feelings. This applies to sentimental items like photographs or other family history types items. Wanting these reminders of the joyous times and people in your life is a goal to celebrate while respecting things.

Taking Action

Storing Sentimental Items

The very nature of sentimental items means you want to store them in a way that honours the memories or people they're connected to. Therefore, simply dumping them in a box, and shoving the parcel in a corner to be forgotten and damaged, is not the way to go. Be deliberate about storing these items so they remain protected and last as long as possible. Let's look at a few everyday sentimental items and how to keep them.

Photographs: Physical photographs are memorabilia that most of us have, and they usually represent special moments, people, and places we want to remember. They're often a visual symbol of our family history or special occasions. A common problem with simply storing your photographs in a stack is that they tend to get stuck together and then peel off once they're exposed to moisture because of the film covering the picture. Start by organizing them into categories. They can be sorted by date, who or what they're off, or by how important they're to you. You can create your time capsule or archive by organizing photographs. Arranging them in a system almost increases their power to make you feel nostalgic because a timeline or category tells a story.

Next, find the storage solution that suits you. You can store them in albums, where a plastic sheet covers each page to preserve the picture.

Another storage option is keeping them loosely but in air-tight and waterproof containers—store photographs and photo albums off the ground and away from excessive heat or water. The attic or garage is usually a suitable storage location for pictures.

Clothes: You might want to treasure your baby's first shoes or your late mom's favourite dress. Store these items in air-tight and waterproof containers, old pillowcases, or spare suit covers inside an extra suitcase to prevent mould from damaging them.

Papers: This category includes letters, certificates, or tickets. Prioritize your unique documents by their type, who they're from, their date, or how special they're to you. These can then be indexed according to your category, and safely stored in their required order in a file, with each page or document in a plastic sleeve to prevent staining or water damage. You can also go the extra mile to preserve these items by having them laminated and then storing them in a handy concertina file according to their category.

Books: These can be stored in air-tight and waterproof containers in your garage, attic, or basement. Avoid them being damaged by keeping them away from dampness. To organize your books for storage, arrange them alphabetically by title or author, by their author, or by the colour of the cover.

Collectors' items: This category includes comic books, model cars, action figures, or ornaments. These items are often valuable; therefore, store them in a way that preserves their good condition. Before you decide to keep the entire collection, consider if one piece can serve as a representation of the whole group. Ask yourself if you need your entire collection or if you would consider selling a few valuable parts to earn a return on what you initially spent.

Store comic books in a stack or upright in sturdy air-tight and waterproof storage bins or boxes. Keep them away from sunlight to prevent them from fading, and remember that cardboard boxes are not waterproof. Comics can be categorized alphabetically by issue, year, or content. Collections of model cars, action figures, or ornaments are best stored in sealable plastic storage bins. Invest in bubble wrap to ensure your items don't break in storage.

Jewelry: Rings, watches, necklaces, bangles, earrings, and any jewelry must be stored at room temperature because these tend to tarnish if they're exposed to extended humidity. Invest in mini storage boxes with drawers and compartments to keep your sentimental jewelry. Cut up a few sponges and use these to line the bottom of your storage containers to prevent your jewelry from getting scratched.

Other Miscellaneous Items: These might include records, CDs, toys, glassware, dishes, kitchen supplies, and stuffed animals. Categorize them by the person or moment they relate to, age, or type (e.g., toys and glassware will form their categories). Store these items in sealable boxes or storage bins and use helpful supplies like bubble wrap or newspaper for dishes and glassware, pillowcases for stuffed animals, and jars or small containers for small items.

Displaying Sentimental Items

If you want to display your sentimental items, make sure that you show them off in a way that indicates that you respect and value them. Avoid placing them in a random corner of your home that you ignore so that they end up dusty and neglected. Choosing to display your sentimental items means that you're also choosing that cleaning them becomes part of your regular organization routine in your home. Failing to move them around, dust them, or wash them if required defeats the purpose of keeping these items.

Start by selecting a space for these items. They can be spread out around your home,
but they must not clutter your space, burden you

with an intense cleaning routine, or get in your way while you spin around your home during your daily routine. A good location is usually the living room, alongside the television stand, or mounted on the walls to create a very personal design element to the room and give it character.

The foyer or entrance hall is another excellent place for sentimental items to be displayed to make your house warm for you and your guests. A popular trend for living rooms and bedrooms is to paint a family tree on your wall as a mural and use family photographs to populate the tree. A nook in the corner of a room, or the mantelpiece above the fireplace, are other locations usually suitable for sentimental items. The site you choose should bring the room together, complement the aesthetic, and focus the attention on the stuff you want to display.

Once you have chosen a location for your sentimental items, select a display vessel to show them off in an organized way. This can be a display case, floating shelves, a wall rack, a bookshelf, a display table, a stylish vintage trunk or chest, or a decorative memory box in the room.

So, you have chosen your display location and display vessel. Now select how you want to display each item.

Display your photographs, concert tickets,

sentimental letters, and other delicate items in albums or differently sized frames. Using a much larger structure than the framed object creates the famous "negative space" aesthetic and draws the focus into the bound. Clear containers, glass jars, or boxes that you have bought or repurposed by decorating can be used to display small items like gemstones, seashells, and other trinkets. Personalized or plain mugs can be an excellent way to show pens or pencils that might be significant to you.

Feel free to categorize your display items by any method you prefer. I have floating shelves in my living room, each displaying items representing an essential person in my life. To start an exciting conversation with your next guest, things like model cars or action figures can be arranged according to colour, type, or brand. You can organize your items by their type, by the year they're from, by the person or occasion they relate to, or just let your creativity flow and choose the most visually appealing way of organizing them.

You kept your sentimental items during the decluttering process because they're significant to you, and you believe they deserve a space in your home. These items should be displayed to reflect how they make you feel about that time or that person. Don't let them become cluttered; cherish them by keeping them organized.

* * *

Key Takeaways from This Chapter

We're about to delve into how to keep your house clean and organized by tailoring your organizing routine to your lifestyle. Before we proceed, let's review how to value and respect our sentimental items.

- pat yourself on the back for making the hard decisions it took to either let go of or keep some of your most sentimental items.
- Sentimental items can include photographs, clothing, journals, letters, artwork, memorabilia, ornaments, toys, cards, books, concert tickets, and collectors' items like comics, action figures, or model cars.
- The memory or emotion connected to a sentimental item is what you're attached to, not the item itself. Cherish the memory and know that these memories can never be taken away from you, nor are they stored in the object.
- Store sentimental items in a way that respects their value and meaning. Invest in air-tight and waterproof storage bins, store them above ground, use bubble wrap to wrap up breakable items, and use photo albums to archive, index, and keep your precious memories. The things can be organized

alphabetically by date, type, content, or colour.

- For collections, consider if you can keep one stand-out or favourite piece that symbolizes the entire group instead of the whole collection.
- When displaying sentimental items, dedicate a space for them, then choose a container, shelf, case, or another vessel to show them. Then, decide how you want to display each item using frames, boxes, or jars. Lastly, organize the space in any order you wish, be creative, and make it memorable for you to look at. Your display should reflect how the items make you feel.

* * *

EXERCISE #10

Show Love to Loved Ones

Date:____________

Choose five important photographs for you and select a place to display them. Pick one sentimental item representing each family member and close friend group and choose a location to display them.

CHAPTER 11: MAINTENANCE AND CLEANING

A place for everything, and everything in its place. –Isabella Mary Beeton

The Basics of Cleaning

Your initial goal was to get control of your life by taking back control of your home and its spaces.

You started this journey by decluttering your home; then, you decluttered your home. In this book, you took on the challenge of organizing your home, and now we are at the final stage, which is maintaining and cleaning your home, so it stays organized. Do you find yourself apologizing to guests when they walk in, even though you have gone through the process of decluttering your home? Does saying "Excuse the mess" and a nervous laugh naturally come to you? This should not be the norm. Organizing your home, and keeping it that way, allows you to be unapologetically house-proud because you know the work you put in to get it neat, tidy, and hygienic.

Essential Cleaning Tools

There are very few people who love cleaning and housework, but we all know that it is a necessity if you want to have peace of mind in your home. I'm not asking you to turn into a Stepford Wife and switch to autopilot to get your house clean. Still, I recommend investing in a few good-quality essentials to ensure your cleaning time is not wasted or futile.

Vacuum Cleaner: Investing in a good quality vacuum cleaner will make your cleaning routine a breeze and allow you to eliminate the dirt that a broom cannot get to. A broom does the job, but a vacuum does the job *well*.

Mop: An excellent old-fashioned spaghetti mop, a

fancy electric steam mop, or a squeegee mop will do just fine. A mop gets rid of any dirt that your vacuum might have missed. You can also add some disinfectant into the water you dip your mop in to disinfect your floors.

Cloths, Swabs and Sponges: Invest in about ten good quality clothes, and Colour-code them by their function, so they stay separate. For example, blue garments are used to clean the bathroom and red for the kitchen. Microfiber cloths do a great job of picking up dust, and cotton cloths can be used to get rid of dirt and grime.

A good quality dishwasher, washing machine, and dryer are also essential to save time and money on your water bill. Their very definition describes the functionality and convenience of these machines because the alternative requires time and hard labour for you.

Detergents

Your house will never be adequately clean without the regular use of detergents. I advise buying them in bulk and decanting them into smaller containers if you have the storage space and time to do so. Buying them in bulk saves you money and multiple trips to the store. Buy a few empty plastic bottles with trigger spray tops to make your detergents last longer.

As a rule of thumb, a five-litre container of bleach should last a family of four people about two months, with a weekly deep-cleaning routine. You can attempt to make your detergents using household substances,. Still, I would be wary of mixing chemicals without proper training unless Breaking Bad inspires your cleaning routine. The following detergents are must-haves around the home:

- Bleach
- Thick bleach for toilets and showers
- Dishwashing liquid
- Laundry detergent
- Fabric softener
- Window cleaner for windows and any other glass surface like mirrors or glass tables
- Furniture polish for wooden furniture
- Furniture oil for leather furniture

To make your cleaning routine run as smoothly as possible, place one bottle of each of the above detergents (except those used for laundry) into a portable trolley, cart, basket, box, or bucket that can be carried around as you clean your home. Running back and forth to your kitchen to fetch different bottles can be exhausting, frustrating, and slow down your cleaning system.

Nice-To-Haves

These items are not essential but will make your life a little easier if you spend a few extra coins and minutes on your cleaning routine. Scented disinfectant is a great way to ensure your house always smells good and serves the dual purpose of disinfecting your floors and countertops. White spirit vinegar is a handy cleaning agent that removes almost all dirt, grease, and grime. Mix a bit with water and keep it in a spray bottle in your kitchen. Mothballs are effective at keeping insects away from any room.

Simply put a few in the corners of each room in your home and replenish them when they dissolve. Lighting incense sticks also helps keep pesky insects like flies and mosquitoes at bay. It also gives your home a pleasant fragrance to create a relaxed and inviting atmosphere. The sanitizer has become popular due to the COVID-19 pandemic, and you might loathe constantly spraying it on your hands, but it can be convenient in your kitchen and bathrooms. Add a few splashes to your mopping water or leave a spray bottle in the bathroom for daily use to make your weekly cleaning much more manageable.

Weekly Cleaning Routine

Make this routine non-negotiable. Incorporate it

into your work, school, and social schedule. Don't compromise on completing this routine because you will regret it if you neglect it, and the clutter and dirt will inevitably build up. Establish a cleaning system that you repeat every week. Allocate the same amount of time to clean the same rooms in the same order. This is the only way the routine will get more accessible, and you will get faster at completing it. From my experience, the average three-bedroom house takes two to three hours to deep-clean every week.

Clean the following areas of your home once a week: kitchen (including your stove, sink, and microwave), bathrooms, bedrooms, living room, home office, garden, entrance hall or foyer, and patio or porch. The room you start in depends on you, but most people prefer to clean their house from one side to the other instead of going in different directions. Use my cleaning method below to get those household chores done in no time:

1. *Wipe*: Start by removing higher surfaces like countertops, shelves, and ceiling fans. Continue to wipe down to the lower items until you reach ground level. Polish your furniture and shine up your glass surfaces at this step. It doesn't make sense to wipe lower surfaces first because dust falls, giving you double the work.

2. *Vacuum*: Next, vacuum the floor of every room in your home in up and down rows. Imagine that you are sweeping across a (very loud) zen garden. Move any furniture that can be moved, and vacuum underneath it. Move your sofa and your bed to avoid dust building up.
3. *Mop*: Grab a bucket of water and put in a splash of bleach, sanitizer, and scented disinfectant, and mop the same way that you vacuumed.
4. *Disinfect*: Get deep into those bacteria-laden areas like the shower, toilet, stove, microwave, and kitchen sink, using regular and thick bleach and scourers to ensure every inch is hygienic. Don't forget to disinfect high-touch areas like the toilet flusher handle and taps.
5. *Relax*: Take a break because you deserve it.

Please make a point of doing your laundry, folding it or ironing it, and putting it away every week. Spend 15 minutes every week walking around your home, picking up things and putting them back where they belong so that they do not become inconvenient clutter if they do have a home.

Don't pause your cleaning routine until it is complete. Be strict about this; you will see actual results in your well-organized home.

Monthly Cleaning Routine

These tasks would be unnecessary every week but still, need to be done. Do a thorough audit of your refrigerator, freezer, and pantry once a month to check for expired food or items that need replenishment on your next trip to the grocery store. Clean your oven at least once a month using a powerful oven cleaner that you spray, leave to work, and wipe off after a few hours. Check your supply of toiletries and cosmetics once a month to find out what you need to buy. Change the linen on your bed every month. Check your home office for filed papers requiring action at least once a month, so you don't miss any payments or deadlines. Rotate your children's toys monthly to keep them stimulated and their space clutter-free. Clean your windows and sliding doors with window cleaner or a vinegar and water mix.

Annual Cleaning Routine

You should ideally review the contents of every space in your home at least once a year. Avoid the stress and panic of leaving every room for the end of the year and stagger it by tackling a room can or when you feel it's time for review. Review the contents of your closet in the middle of the year, when the weather starts to warm up or cool down, depending on where you are in the world. Reorganize or reposition your sentimental items on display, so you don't get tired of looking at them.

As a rule, you should eliminate one thing for every new item brought into your closet. Clean and reorganize your garage, attic, and basement before the holidays to get to those decorations quickly. Make decluttering part of your annual cleaning routine so that you can control your home and stay in an orderly and organized condition.

* * *

Key Takeaways from This Chapter

Deciding on your maintenance and cleaning routine is the final step in your journey to an entire organized home, so a quick recap is required before we reflect on your organizing journey as a whole.

- Your like or dislike of cleaning has nothing to do with the fact that it has to be done for your home to remain organized.
- Invest in a good quality vacuum cleaner, mop, cloths, swabs, dishwasher, washing machine, and dryer to make cleaning hassle-free.
- Detergents are necessary to clean every part of your home. Ensure you keep the following: bleach, dishwashing liquid, thick bleach, window cleaner, and furniture polish.
- Your weekly cleaning routine must involve

cleaning your house from one side to the other using the four-step method of wiping, vacuuming, mopping, and disinfecting.

- Monthly cleaning routines involve checking for expired food, replenishing toiletries, changing your linen, cleaning your oven, and cleaning your windows.
- Once a year, you should clean out your basement, garage, and attic and review the contents of your closet.
- Organizing is an ongoing process that requires a system and dedication.

* * *

EXERCISE #11

Ready, Set, Clean!

Date:___________

Give yourself one week to research, source and buy all your cleaning essential tools and detergents. On your cleaning day, set a timer for 180 minutes, and challenge yourself to clean your house before the timer runs out.

EXERCISE #12

Annual Review

Date:____________

Make a list of items you would consider getting rid of if you haven't used them once in six months. Keep this list safe so you can use it when decluttering at the end of the year

CONCLUSION

Be grateful for the home you have, knowing that at this moment, all you have is all you need. –Sarah Ban Breathnach

Statistics show that "in 2021, the market size of the home organizing industry has reached approximately $11.4 billion, and it is expected to grow over the next few years" (Peysakhovich, 2022). This shows that people are concerned enough with decluttering and organizing their homes to spend a part of their income on it. This is progress because it indicates a shift in their mindset from associating happiness with accumulating stuff to realizing that happiness is found in respecting and valuing your things.

The above sentiments are precisely where we began this journey of organizing your home with a transformation of your mindset. Understanding the difference between decluttering and organizing are keys to embarking on your journey to an organized home. You would have already decluttered your home and your mind by applying the principles in the first three books in my *Happy Decluttered Life* series. After completing the decluttering process, you can hopefully see that simply having less stuff gives you more control over the running of your home. Remember that you are not your clutter, you are not your untidiness, and these are issues that can be easily fixed by applying my techniques.

We explored the benefits of increasing your self-awareness with the *EQ Wheel* to overcome negative thoughts of self-doubt you might have about organizing your home. Remain goal-oriented and be firm in your decisions about organizing your home. Remember to be kind to yourself; acknowledge the contributing factors to your negative thoughts and be willing to overcome them by seeing the light at the end of the disorganized tunnel.

The above sentiments are precisely where we began this journey of organizing your home with a transformation of your mindset. Understanding the difference between decluttering and organizing is key to embarking on your journey to an organized home. You would have already decluttered your home and your mind by applying the principles in the first three books in my *Happy Decluttered Life* series.

After completing the decluttering process, you can hopefully see that simply having less stuff gives you more control over the running of your home. Remember that you are not your clutter; you are not your untidiness, and these are issues that can be easily fixed by applying my techniques.

The next mountain to conquer was learning to develop good organizing habits and routines based on your family structure and lifestyle. To successfully get rid of your bad habits and replace them with good ones, you have to ask yourself what you should stop doing, what you should continue doing, and what you should start doing. Checklists, to-do lists, calendars, and chalkboards are your friends.

They can make organizing much more enjoyable through that feeling of achievement, of crossing something off your list as complete. Developing good home management habits is essential because organizing is not a once-off activity; it is an ongoing process that must be incorporated as a necessity to improve your lifestyle.

We then explored methods to overcome

procrastination, the infamous waster of time. These methods are framed around a few common threads; namely:

- Always be clear about your goals.

- Prioritize the steps or actions you need to take to achieve your goals.

- Focus on your strengths to complete your tasks.

- Be your motivator, and don't start a new task until you complete the one at hand.

Unpacking the basics of organizing was necessary to lay a solid foundation for achieving your goals at home. To determine how to organize your home, you must consider the challenges, needs, wants, and actions you need to take to begin organizing a space. The basics include choosing an organization system and a theme to categorize items within that system.

Remember to assess the area before purchasing storage containers. The space you organize first should depend on the rooms you use the most. I provided practical tips on how to organize every space and item in your home, including the kitchen, refrigerator, freezer, bathroom, living room, dining room, patio, backyard, kids' playroom, den, home office, bedroom, linen, dressing area, closet, garage, basement, attic, and your sentimental items.

Always prioritize making the best use of your space, especially vertical space, and organize it so that it's easy for you to keep everything dust-free and hygienic.

The final step in controlling your home is keeping the spaces organized and clean. My cleaning routine of wiping, vacuuming, mopping, and disinfecting will work for every room in your house. Allocating a block of time for cleaning, sticking to that time, and doing the required tasks every week, month, or year will allow you to live in your heaven.

People waste time searching for everyday items, and surveys indicate that "most people estimate that they could save close to an hour just by being better organized" (Peysakhovich, 2022). An extra hour in your day can change your life in many ways, and you can master more than you ever thought by being able to spend time on yourself and your loved ones instead of searching for things.When you put down this book, I hope you are inspired to take back control of your life and home by realizing that you have the power over your space, not the other way around. Focus on the stuff you kept instead of what you got rid of, and remember to give each room a character or flare that is unique to you. Replace stress with peace of mind, replace chores with quality time, replace procrastination with action, adjust your lens from focusing on your stuff to concentrating on your life, and reap the benefits of getting organized.

Kai

* * *

MORE FROM THE AUTHOR

Thank You

I would like to really thank you for reading my book till the end, and most importantly, apply as much as you can from what you learned here. As nothing would make me happier than knowing that someone's life is getting better because of something I shared!

I consider myself leveraged because you chose my book over all the other books to discover.

So, THANK YOU for purchasing this book and for making it all the way to here.

Before you leave, I would like to ask for a favour! **Could you please share one or two things you learned or liked about this book in a review? That would really help me continue sharing more knowledge and would show your support to an independent author like myself!**

Your opinion will assist and encourage me to keep writing and publishing useful content to more people, hoping to make more people happier and enjoy their dream lives. Hearing from you would mean so much to me.

>> Leave a review on Amazon US <<

>> Leave a review on Amazon UK <<

REFERENCES

Aarssen, C. (n.d.). *ClutterBug.* https://clutterbug.me/cas-aarssen

Abramson, A. (2022 February 4). *7 Pro Tips for Organizing Your Tiny Bedroom. Apartment Therapy.* https://www.apartmenttherapy.com/small-bedroom-organizing-tips-37031030

Avila Uribe, L. (2022 April 7). *Get your life together with these must-have bathroom organizing essentials.* HuffPost. https://www.huffpost.com/entry/organize-bathroom-cabinets-shelves_l_624c6bdfe4b0d8266ab1e133

Barber, M. (2020 March 19). *Why home organizing is my coronavirus coping tool.* Curbed. https://archive.curbed.com/2020/3/19/21185734/coronavirus-anxiety-tips-home-organization

Block, C. (2020 May 18). *6 Organizing Style Personalities & How To Stay*

Organized For Life. Sane Spaces. https://sanespaces.com/2020/05/organize-types-organize-styles-stay-organized-for-life/

Boone, L. (2020 March 27). *Expert tips on decluttering your home during the coronavirus pandemic.* Los Angeles Times. https://www.latimes.com/lifestyle/story/2020-03-27/expert-tips-on-decluttering-your-home-during-the-coronavirus

Burns, L. (2022 February 18). *10 organization quotes to live by.* Organized-Ish. https://www.lelaburris.com/organization-quotes/

Cherry, K. (2020 May 30). *The psychology behind why we wait until the last minute to do things.* Verywell Mind. https://www.verywellmind.com/the-psychology-of-procrastination-2795944

ClutterBug (2021). *How to stop procrastinating and really get motivated* [YouTube Video]. https://www.youtube.com/watch?v=x3EYb6OEqB0&ab_channel=ClutterBug

Decoraid. (n.d.). *15 living room organization tips we swear by.* Interior Design Guide. https://www.decoraid.com/blog/living-room-organization/

DePaul, K. (2021 February 2). *What does it really*

take to build a new habit? Harvard Business Review. https://hbr.org/2021/02/what-does-it-really-take-to-build-a-new-habit

Eatough, E. (2021 December 7). *Building good habits in your life (and ditching bad ones).* BetterUp. https://www.betterup.com/blog/building-habits

Eisenberg, R. (2021 July 26). *A simple 5-step plan to organize your sentimental items quick, easy & done.* The Organizing Confessions. https://blog.ronnieisenberg.com/2021/07/26/a-simple-5-step-plan-to-organize-your-sentimental-items-quick-easy-done/#.Yol4qKhBzrd

Elaine, C. (2020). *Small kitchen organization on a budget 2020/ renter friendly kitchen organization hacks & ideas* [YouTube Video]. https://www.youtube.com/watch?v=2_VDqSmVncI&ab_channel=CatherineElaine

Emily, O. (2021 December 11). *How to organize a kitchen – a simple guide to clear the clutter.* Livingetc. https://www.livingetc.com/advice/how-to-organize-a-kitchen

Garrity, A., & Thomas, M. (2022 April 4). *40 unique kitchen organization ideas for easy access and clutter-free storage.* Good Housekeeping. https://www.goodhousekeeping.com/home/organizing/tips/g1397/small-kitchen-storage/?slide=1

Geddes, J. K. (2022 May 4). *5 types of clutter even professional organizers have in their attics, basements, and beyond.* Realtor. https://www.realtor.com/advice/home-improvement/basement-and-garage-clutter-spots-you-must-tackle-now/

Halton, C. (2022 April 27). *15 brilliant organising quotes to help you get sorted out!* Organise My House. https://organisemyhouse.com/organising-quotes/

Hauser, E. (2021 August 21). *Why the Home Edit Method Is Perfect for 2021.* Life Savvy. https://www.lifesavvy.com/88909/why-the-home-edit-method-is-perfect-for-2021/

Hidlebaugh, E. (2021a May 16). *Toy rotation categories didn't fix our toy mess, so we did this instead!* Minimize My Mess. https://www.minimizemymess.com/blog/toy-rotation

Hidlebaugh, E. (2021b October 31). *How to organize your home in 30 days.* Minimize My Mess. https://www.minimizemymess.com/blog/organize-your-home-in-30-days

Hidlebaugh, E. (2021 April 3). *79 Inspiring Home Organization Quotes.* Minimize My Mess. https://www.minimizemymess.com/blog/organized-quotes

Justice, Dr. I., & Target Training International, Ltd. (2021). *Emotional Quotient.* In ORCA HR Solutions. https://www.orcahrsolutions.com/wp-content/uploads/2021/05/TTI-Emotional-Quotient-EQ.pdf

KonMari. (n.d.). *About the KonMari method.* KonMari. https://konmari.com/about-the-konmari-method/

Konstantinides, A. (2020,May 12). *13 tricks for organizing your clothes, according to an expert who transforms celebrity closets.* Insider. https://www.insider.com/how-to-clean-your-closet-tips-professional-organizer

La Sala, C., & McAuliffe, R. (2022 March 15). *20 bathroom storage ideas perfect for your 2022 spring cleaning needs.* New York Post. https://nypost.com/article/bathroom-storage-ideas/

Lally, P., van Jaarsveld, C. H. M., Potts, H. W. W., & Wardle, J. (2009). How are habits formed: Modelling habit formation in the real world. *European Journal of Social Psychology*, 40(6), 998–1009. https://doi.org/10.1002/ejsp.674

Martin, B. (2021 April 28). *15 secrets to cleaning your home in half the time.* Popular Mechanics. https://www.popularmechanics.com/home/interior-projects/how-to/g1238/15-secrets-to-cleaning-your-home-in-half-the-time/

Mindful Staff. (2020 July 8). *What is mindfulness?* Mindful. https://www.mindful.org/what-is-mindfulness/

Monte, S. (n.d.). *Bathroom organizing ideas you likely won't find anywhere else.* Elegant Simplicity. https://elegantsi.com/blog/bathroom-organizing-ideas

Novak, J., & tasteofhome.com. (2022 January 5). *20 home organizing mistakes you're probably making (and how to fix them!*. Reader's Digest Canada. https://www.readersdigest.ca/home-garden/cleaning/things-professional-organizers-dont-do-at-home/

Nystul, J. (2021 August 28). *15 easy ways to make your living room more organized.* One Good Thing. https://www.onegoodthingbyjillee.com/fall-organizing-week-family-room/

Peysakhovich, R. (2022 January 16). *51 home organizing industry statistics & trends for 2022.* Onedesk. https://www.getonedesk.com/home-organizing-statistics

Picard, C., & Kirby, N. (2021 February 23). *45 home quotes for all the homebodies out there. House Beautiful.* https://www.housebeautiful.com/lifestyle/fun-at-home/g15064764/home-quotes/?slide=1

Poplin, J. (2018). *The difference between decluttering and organizing.* The Simplicity Habit. https://www.thesimplicityhabit.com/the-difference-between-decluttering-and-organizing/

Say, J. (2020 September 21). *67 motivational habit quotes (power of routine).* Gracious Quotes. https://graciousquotes.com/habit-quotes/

Scandish Home. (2022). *42 tips to have an organized and clean home| whole house organizing | homemaking* [YouTube Video]. https://www.youtube.com/watch?v=Ep6d6ore4-I&ab_channel=ScandishHome

Schiller, A., & Boisvert, M. (2020 October 21). *The 4 main types of procrastinators and how to not be one of them, according to 2 accountability coaches.* Business Insider South Africa. https://www.businessinsider.co.za/main-types-of-procrastinators-how-to-avoid-accountability-coaches?r=US&IR=T

St. John, N. (2015 July 24). *Why procrastination is the thief of time.* HuffPost. https://www.huffpost.com/entry/why-procrastination-is-th_b_7854176

The Lockup. (2020 October 13). *What to Store in the Attic, Basement or Garage?* The Lockup. https://news.thelockup.com/what-to-store-in-your-attic-basement-and-garage/

The Sunday Stylist. (2019). *10 tips for a clean and tidy home - simple habits for an organized home* [YouTube Video]. https://www.youtube.com/watch?v=72CaIK3Uefc&ab_channel=THESUNDAYSTYLIST

Tracy, B. (2006). *Eat that frog! : 21 great ways to stop procrastinating and get more done in less time* (2nd ed). Berrett-Koehler.

Vasseur, B. (2017). *Small Bathroom Organization Ideas!* [YouTube Video]. https://www.youtube.com/watch?v=TCZxpcPcQ0c&ab_channel=BrittanyVasseur

Manufactured by Amazon.ca
Bolton, ON

29229563R00109